TEAMWORK

Instant

TEAMWORK

Motivate & energize your team NOW!

Brian Clegg
Paul Birch

KOGAN PAGE

This edition published in 2009

Kogan Page India Private Limited
4737/23 Ansari Road,
Daryaganj
New Delhi 110 002

This edition is for sale in the Indian subcontinent only. Not for export elsewhere.

ISBN-10: 81-7554-435-X
ISBN-13: 978-81-7554-435-2

Published by Vinod Vasishtha for Kogan Page India Private Limited,
4737/23, Ansari Road, Daryaganj, New Delhi 110 002.

Printed and bound by Raj Press, R-3, Inderpuri, New Delhi - 110 012.

Contents

1

THE NEED

INSTANT TEAMWORK

This book is packed with extremely quick exercises to enhance teamwork. You haven't time? That's no excuse. You stand to lose a lot more than the five minutes spent on one of these exercises if you are not getting the best from your team. Perhaps your team, your group, or your course is perfect. Maybe. But if so, you are unique. For the rest of us, we have a potentially powerful resource in a team. Like most powerful resources it needs tuning. Hence 'instant teamwork'.

YOU'VE BEEN THERE

You have pulled together a new team. They're nervous. They don't know each other. They don't really know what their role is. They need something to break down the barriers and get started. Or perhaps your team is well established, but it lacks a certain drive. Team meetings are dull with a capital D. You know that everyone could contribute more.

It's day one of the training course. Half of your audience are reading newspapers. The other half are looking as if they'd rather be somewhere else.

You have brought together a cross-functional group to attack a serious business problem. Everyone knows what the problem is, but no one knows how to get started. You need something to boost the creative energy.

Are these examples familiar? They ought to be. We've all been there. Whether you are running a team or are part of it, whether you are involved in a meeting, training or a problem solving session, so often there's something that's not quite right. What you need is a quick fix.

SYNERGY OR DISRUPTION

Everyone knows that teams are great. Just try using 'teamwork' as an insult; it won't work. Every management text, every football game commentary, every corporate communication hammers in the message – the team is the ideal. Contrast 'team player' and 'loner' – which would you rather see on your performance report? Yet look at most real teams and you will see something less than perfect.

The theoretical benefit of a team can be summed up in one word – synergy. Synergy was originally a biological term, describing the way a combination of different parts of a body could provide more than simply the sum of the parts. More recently it has come to apply to a group of people in a similar way. Teamwork is supposed to combine the talents of the individuals to produce something more than is possible with each individual taken separately. We can all think of examples where this is true. But equally, it is possible to think of cases where the pulling together of a team has a negative effect.

'Teams' may have very positive overtones, but 'committees' (a camel is a horse designed by committee) and 'meetings' ('not another meeting; all I do is go from one meeting to another') are very different.

All too often the result of pulling together a group of people is not to provide synergy but disruption. At best, the result is to bore everyone into minimal contribution. At worst, there will be active suppression of new ideas and blatant time wasting. Does this mean that all the hype about teams is mistaken? In certain circumstances, yes. There are some activities that simply work better when undertaken by an individual. But generally, and certainly in the business context, teams can bring real benefits. The trouble is, how can you get the team working together? It would help to know what is keeping it apart.

THE NATURE OF THE BEAST

A team is a collection of individuals. Always. This is one of those self-evident truths that is very easy to ignore most of the time. It is very convenient to think of a team as a unit, as a single entity. It implies focus and control. But it's a convenient fiction; it just isn't true. The underlying individuality is essential. It's the reason you get synergy at all. If everyone thought and acted exactly the same way, you wouldn't get anything different (apart from increased physical contribution) from 10 people than from one. Unfortunately, individuality is also a problem. It means that a new group will function poorly because other members seem strange. We treat them cautiously until they are familiar. There is a need to break down the barriers – not removing individuality, but increasing comfort with being together.

Groups of people are very good at picking up and amplifying mood. If there is a slight feeling of boredom, or of low energy, before long the whole team is drooping. Performance collapses. There's a need for a boost. Sometimes this can be physiological. Stimulants like coffee, sugar boosters like sweets and biscuits, can give a quick lift. But these are nowhere near as effective as finding a mechanism for increasing group energy.

Groups of people also fall into ruts. That's the problem with brainstorming. It is very easy to get stuck in a particular line of thinking or to get tunnel vision. Despite synergy, groups can actually reinforce tunnel vision by suppressing anyone who comes up with a different idea. One dominant individual can also steamroller a group in a particular direction. Often there's a need to take a step back from the process, to be pushed for a moment into thinking in a different way. When the group returns to the problem, this activity should have moved them far enough from their preconceptions to get moving again.

These three requirements: ice-breakers to break down barriers between people; warm-ups to increase energy; and time-outs to change the direction of thinking, are the basis of this book. They aren't miracle cures for a sick team, but they deliver the sort of boost that high energy drinks claim to give athletes.

'INSTANT' IS ESSENTIAL

The 'instant' in the title is no accident. Unless these exercises are very quick they are self-defeating. They get in the way instead of helping. Similarly, they should be available at a moment's notice. You can predict that you will need an ice-breaker at the start of a session with a new team, or that you might need to warm up a group after lunch, but often the best use of these exercises is reactive. Everyone's flagging – let's throw in a warm-up. We're getting bogged down, let's have a time-out. Then the instant nature of the exercises comes into play. Instant teamwork is a first-aid kit as well as a planned health boost.

SILLY GAMES

There may be some resistance to using these exercises. They are seen as being silly games. It's not surprising – many of them are. Some would not be out of place at a children's party. But why is that a problem? If it is, it shows a lack of understanding of people. In engineering a change to the way a team works, we are acting at a low level. Although the team's tasks may be entirely cerebral, the interaction between team members is much more at the gut level. Similarly, the development of ideas may be very logical and thought-through, but the original creative spark is something deeper and darker. Is it really surprising, then, that the activities that are needed to improve teamwork operate at a similarly basic level? The fact is, cerebral activity tends to lower energy and interaction rather than increasing them. Like it or not, you need to get down to basics to improve teamworking.

You may appreciate this, but still have members of the group who don't; who refuse take part because 'it's silly' or 'it's not what I'm here for'. If this happens, it is important not to ignore them. Give everyone else a two-minute tea break and take the individual to one side. Explain the scientific reasoning for working at a gut level. If this fails, appeal to their team spirit – they don't have to like it, but please just go along with it to humour everyone else. If you still fail (and it's rare), you may have to consider removing them from the group. Their actions could make their contribution so negative that the team will function more effectively without them.

THE REAL THING

Instant teamwork isn't going to work miracles, but by using it in the two ways described – as a planned resource to break the ice and to energize, and as a first-aid kit when energy droops or you get into a rut – it will make a huge contribution. You are going to improve the effectiveness of your team, the quality of your output and perhaps best of all, the fun of taking part.

2

THE EXERCISES

WHAT'S INSIDE

After this second short introductory chapter you reach the meat of *Instant Teamwork* – the exercises. Each comes in a standard format, beginning with some basic information: any preparation required, the time the exercise will take, environmental requirements and team size restrictions. Next is the exercise itself, with notes on feedback, the outcome and possible variations. Finally there is a star rating to help match a specific exercise to your requirements.

WHERE'S THE TEAMWORK?

It might seem strange in a book called *Instant Teamwork* that some of the exercises have a low star rating for team building. In fact all the exercises, whether undertaken individually or as a group, are designed to enhance teamwork in one particular session. However, some activities are particularly strong on reinforcing long-term team strengths, and it is these which score high on the team building category.

AN ARTIFICIAL DIVIDE

The exercises are divided into three sections: ice-breakers, warm-ups and time-outs. These match the three requirements we have already discussed. However, the divisions are frankly arbitrary. A good ice-breaker will also often provide an effective warm-up. A time-out that is stimulating creativity will frequently increase energy as a warm-up does. For this reason, in the Appendix we have some quick reference tables. If you are looking for a high energy exercise, the high energy table will point you straight to the appropriate exercises. Whether you stick to our categories or not is up to you; use the book the way it works best for you.

ICE-BREAKERS

The first section deals with exercises which are designed to break down the barriers between people, whether you are dealing with a new team, a group of people from different parts of the company (or the world), or simply a new, unfamiliar situation. Nervousness, shyness and inhibitions can all be barriers to effective teamwork.

One style of ice-breaker acts at the social level. Here we find out a little more about the other people in the group. Their names, their interests, what they do in their spare time. This is an accelerated version of normal social interaction, moving the team members from strangers to part of your social grouping. Other ice-breakers are physical, putting people in close physical proximity and forcing them to interact. Because this is unacceptable with strangers, the other team members are automatically forced from being 'them' to being 'us'.

WARM-UPS

The whole purpose of a warm-up is to increase group energy. Whatever the purpose of the team, it will be more productive if the members have high energy levels. The two key mechanisms of a warm-up are physical activity and laughter. By their nature, business teams are largely sedentary, often working in over-heated offices with less than perfect air conditioning. The physical side of warm-ups helps counter the numbing effect of the environment. It is sometimes enough just to get people out of their seats, or out of the building, for a minute or two. But there is more to the physical aspect. Activity stimulates the body, and hence the brain into more effective action, not just countering lethargy but positively increasing effectiveness.

The second factor, laughter, is easily disregarded. We are, after all, involved in a serious business. Yet laughter is a powerful force for building energy. Many of the warm-up exercises will stimulate the team members to laugh – at their own ideas and actions, and at others' attempts. This laughter is a very positive force in overcoming lethargy and enhancing productivity.

TIME-OUTS

We have all been in situations where we are trying to work something out, to solve a problem. There's just no way to do it. It's impossible. So you put the problem to one side for a little while and do something different. Somehow, when you come back to it, a new angle becomes visible. The problem isn't quite as intractable as you thought.

This approach has a more general application to creativity. It has been conclusively proved that a short distraction, dealing with something completely different, will improve an individual or a group's creativity when dealing with a particular problem. It shouldn't be surprising. The distraction provides a new starting point, a new viewpoint, when returning to the problem.

This is the basis for the time-out. When the team has become bogged down, when it is lacking creativity, when it needs some inspiration, a time-out can help break out of the tunnel of habitual thought. It is sometimes hard to do. Team members may argue that you are breaking their concentration – they want to get on with the job. But when you are marching towards a dead end, it's well worth the time taken to look in a totally different direction.

PREPARATION

As much as possible, these exercises require no preparation. Sometimes there will be simple props, usually items that can be found around any office environment, but such requirements are kept to a minimum. This is essential to maintain the instant nature of the exercises, but don't ignore those that do need a little work. Sometimes props can make an exercise considerably more powerful. There's something special about using something physical, something you can touch. For that reason, there is a short section of exercises involving technology or other longer preparation. They won't always be useful but they are particularly striking.

For scheduled exercises, preparation will not be a problem. Yet even an off-the-cuff exercise can be planned. You might not know that you'll want a time-out at three o'clock in the afternoon, but you can have a time-out ready for when you do need it. Even if you haven't one planned, if the exercise has only limited preparation, you can send your team members on a five-minute stretch break while you get ready. But there remain plenty of exercises which need no more than your people and this book. The choice is yours.

PRIZES

It is by no means essential, but it can help the effectiveness of an exercise to have prizes. It doesn't matter how old we are, there's something exciting about competing for a prize. It gives an extra urgency to a task, a concrete goal, rather than the airy-fairy one of improving teamwork. However, they do need to be used with care. Generally, the prize should be trivial, so that those who don't win will not feel slighted. Small silly prizes – stocking fillers – go down well. A useful catch-all is a few bags of sweets which contain lots of smaller packets. These have the double benefit of giving a sugar boost too, and you can usually engineer the exercise to give a prize to each group or individual, so there's no divisiveness.

3

ICE-BREAKERS

3.1 *This is my friend*

Preparation None.
Running time One minute per team member.
Environment Standard room format, provided everyone can see the other people present. Circular or U-shaped tables are probably best.
Teams Individual; group can be any size that can sit around in a circle.

Each member of the group takes a turn at introducing the person next to them. They have 60 seconds to tell the rest of the group about the other person. The subject's name should be accurate, but everything else should be made up. You might like to give the group a few minutes to generate ideas first, or the rest of the group will still be constructing their own introduction, rather than listening to their colleagues.

Feedback The more bizarre the association, the better the chance of remembering the person's name, especially if the name is repeated several times throughout the exercise. Be creative, but be aware of possible embarrassment.

Outcome This is a pure ice-breaker. It serves two purposes. The need to introduce someone by name will increase awareness of that name, particularly with the person doing the introducing – if the introduction is special enough, the name may well stick with many of the others too. The exercise also helps break down initial inhibitions by making the participants do something slightly silly, but very low risk.

Variations To increase the power of this exercise as an ice-breaker, and to add to the fun, you can set various limits. For example, there must be at least 10 statements about the individual and the whole thing can't take more than 60 seconds. The other participants can be issued with a weapon in case the person talking falters or goes over time: perhaps soft balls or a water pistol (see Chapter 6 for more information). It will also happen occasionally that something true is said about a subject by accident – again this could be picked up on and used as an excuse to pelt or soak the participant.

Team building	✪✪
Ice-breaking	✪✪✪✪
Energy	✪✪
Creativity	✪✪
Fun	✪✪✪✪

3.2 Tower of Babel

Preparation Two A4 (or letter) pads, two flip-chart markers.
Running time Five minutes.
Environment Enough open space for all participants to stand in. Chairs and tables would be helpful.
Teams Two teams with a minimum total of 10 people.

Split the group into two teams of the same size (with a large group, it doesn't matter too much if one is bigger than the other). The exercise is a race against time. Each person in the two teams must write the number of letters in their first name on a piece of paper. They then must arrange themselves in a group, in such a way that their heads are in descending order of name length – short names highest, long names lowest, same length same height. Each person should be holding the sheet of paper with their name length in their teeth. All sheets must be legible from the front. No feet or knees must be touching the floor or floor covering.

Feedback Be prepared to restart a team which hasn't complied fully with the rules. With a largish group there will be the need to use chairs and/or tables to gain height towards the back. Don't discourage this.

Outcome This activity could fit equally well as a warm-up or a time-out. We've included it as an ice-breaker because it involves some communication between the teams about names, and the close physical interaction is helpful for ice-breaking.

Variations With less than 10 people you could run this in a single team against some arbitrary time limit. Obviously this depends on the number of people – around one minute would work with nine people. Although it is not essential, this is an excellent activity to use an instant camera (see Chapter 6 for more on using instant cameras). A photograph of each team makes an excellent talking point for coffee breaks, while scanned copies of the photographs (or electronic pictures) can be incorporated in post-event feedback to good effect.

Team building	✪✪✪
Ice-breaking	✪✪✪
Energy	✪✪✪
Creativity	✪✪
Fun	✪✪✪✪

3.3 Yes!

Preparation None.
Running time One minute.
Environment Enough open space for all participants to stand in a circle.
Teams Single group, no restrictions.

Get everyone to stand in a circle holding hands. Ask them to crouch down. Explain that you are going to say 'yes', 'yes', 'yes' rhythmically, each time getting slightly louder and slightly higher until you end up with the group jumping into the air shouting 'YES!' Do it.

Feedback Explain that this probably makes them feel very silly – and that's not a bad thing. There are two reasons for this. One is that we often feel silly when coming up with new ideas and original thinking. As you want them to be original and innovative, they need to overcome this resistance to feeling silly. Practice helps – this is a primer in silliness. The second reason for undertaking the exercise is to put the group into a more positive frame of mind. Even if the participants feel absolutely ludicrous, they will get a warm glow and a feeling of shared purpose out of the totally positive nature of the content.

Outcome As with many ice-breakers, there are warm-up and time-out components here. It's important that you give the feedback explaining the reasoning, otherwise some participants (particularly from feeling-suppressing cultures like the British) will feel negative about it. Given that feedback, you should have introduced some energy, made them aware of a possible creativity killer and brought them closer together.

Variations It is a good move to repeat the exercise after the feedback. Now that the participants know the reasons behind what they are doing, they will feel more positive and get more out of the exercise. This variation is positively recommended, if time is available (this is, after all, a very quick exercise). To enhance the ice-breaking aspect you can have everyone's names stuck on them as they take part – the situation will to some extent reinforce retention of names.

Team building	✪✪✪
Ice-breaking	✪✪✪
Energy	✪✪✪
Creativity	✪
Fun	✪✪

3.4 Something for the weekend

Preparation None.
Running time 30 seconds per team member.
Environment Standard room format, provided everyone can see the other participants. Circular or U-shaped tables are probably best.
Teams Individual; group can be any size that can sit around in a circle.

Each member of the group writes down their name and something they did at the weekend. This should be true, but as odd as possible. They pass this on to the person on their right. Starting at an arbitrary position, a participant introduces the person on their left to the group and says what that person did at the weekend. The next person on the right then introduces the person on their left, says what that person did at the weekend, and also repeats the original information. As you move around the group there is a longer and longer chain of information about people round the table.

Feedback Associating an activity, particularly if it is strange, with an individual will help pin their name to them, as will repetition.

Outcome Like 'This is my friend' (3.1), this is primarily designed to get a new group more familiar with each others' names. The weekend activity will also give a pocket insight into a different aspect of the individual than may be seen in a work context. This can be a valuable insight when involved in creative work.

Variations With groups larger than about 10, you might like to restart the chain every tenth person, so the burden is not too large for later starters. Run simply, people who come late in the chain don't get the same level of reinforcement, as their names aren't repeated as often. When you have worked around the table, consider passing the slip with the information two places to the left, so it is now on the left of the person it describes. Make sure that the person who was talked about last is now the first to be described: this way they get extra repetition.

Team building	✪✪
Ice-breaking	✪✪✪✪
Energy	✪✪
Creativity	✪✪
Fun	✪✪✪

3.5 Follow my leader

Preparation Two lists of participants' names, one in a random, non-alphabetical order, numbered from top to bottom, and the other divided into individual slips of paper, numbered in the same order as the random sheet.
Running time Five minutes plus.
Environment Room for the participants to stand up.

Start by making sure your name lists match the participants, without giving away who is who. During the exercise no one should wear a name badge, or use their own name. Give each member of the group a slip of paper with someone else's name on. They must not let go of this slip. The object of the exercise is for the team to end up standing in line in the order you have on your list (based on the numbering on the slips – your list is not on display). Reinforce the fact that no one must use their own name in any way.

Feedback There are two requirements here – to get the names into the right order and to match names to the individuals. Find out how the team decided what to do – was there any discussion, or did people just plunge in? Was there are a concerted tactic? How effective was it?

Outcome This exercise works best with large numbers. The less the group knows each other, the more effective it is. It won't result in everyone knowing everyone else's name, but the names will be familiar, and they should know at least one very well. There is superb chaos as everyone shouts out the name on their slip.

Variations This works best as a group exercise, but it is possible to split into teams. This may be necessary if the group is extremely large. Bear in mind, though, that the exact attendees of any event on the day may be different from your list. Having several lists makes the initial administration more tricky. A minor variant is to finish with the group calling out their names in order – it reinforces the names and helps you to check they've succeeded.

Team building	✪✪✪
Ice-breaking	✪✪✪✪
Energy	✪✪✪
Creativity	✪✪
Fun	✪✪✪✪

3.6 Spoon and string

Preparation For each team, a dessert spoon firmly attached to a long length of string (2 metres per team member).
Running time Five minutes.
Environment Enough room for the participants to all stand up in the same space.
Teams Two or more; at least four or five people per team.

Give each team a spoon and string. In a race against time, the winning team is the first one to have the spoon tied to the other end of the string (putting the team in a bundle), with the string passing up and down alternate sets of clothes of the team members. The string must pass through at least one upper body garment and at least one lower body garment to comply. Warn the participants of the dangers of friction burns if the string is pulled through too fast.

Feedback Have small prizes for each team which manages to compete the exercise, with slightly less interesting prizes each time, so there is an incentive to keep going when the first team has finished. Feel free to comment both during and after the exercise on any interesting positions, use of garments, strange comments made by the participants and so forth. As it is much easier to get the spoon down than up, ask how the team decided who would pass it up their garments.

Outcome This is a high energy exercise, but qualifies as an ice-breaker because it brings the participants into very close physical contact, and also because the need to think about just where the string is passing inevitably breaks down some of the coldness and barriers which may be present initially. The ice-breaking effect continues as the string is removed. At one time a popular party ice-breaker, this is just as effective with business groups.

Variations Particularly sadistic operatives of this exercise might like to keep the spoons in a refrigerator until shortly before starting, maximizing discomfort. It is probably advisable not to use a freezer.

Team building	✪✪
Ice-breaking	✪✪✪✪
Energy	✪✪✪
Creativity	✪✪
Fun	✪✪✪✪

3.7 Piggyback plus

Preparation One blindfold per team; setting up obstacle course.
Running time Five minutes.
Environment Room to set up an obstacle course that one person from each team can go round simultaneously.
Teams Two or more; relatively small overall group.

The exercise is a relay piggyback race. The group is split into even-numbered teams (if odd, one person goes twice). Each person either carries one other member of the team on their back, or is carried, around an obstacle course. When they return to the start, the next pair from their team leaves. The person doing the carrying is blindfolded, leaving the rider to direct them. The blindfold is the baton – the second pair can't leave until the first is back and the second mount has been blindfolded. The obstacle course can be anything from a complex course to simply negotiating the tables and chairs in a meeting room. It doesn't matter if space is tight in places, provided all the teams can race at the same time, and there are places where they can pass each other.

Feedback Encourage teams to shout for their riders, building up the atmosphere and making it harder for rider and mount to communicate. A small prize for the winning team will be appreciated. Find out from the successful team how the riders and mounts communicated. Get some feedback from the whole group as to how the exercise felt.

Outcome There's lots of movement and noise in this exercise, all conducive to increased energy when later contributing to the session. The ice-breaking works on two levels, pulling together the team but also specifically the rider and mount.

Variations The easiest variation is the degree of communication between rider and mount. Try the exercise with no speaking allowed. In the basic form, everyone is either a rider or a mount: you could require each person to take both roles. Make sure with this approach that you don't have a heavy team with one very light person in it. You must also make it clear that anyone is free to sit out. For instance, it would be unwise to insist that a pregnant woman took part.

Team building	✪✪✪
Ice-breaking	✪✪✪
Energy	✪✪✪✪
Creativity	✪
Fun	✪✪✪

3.8 Row of eyes

Preparation None.
Running time Five minutes.
Environment Space to arrange the group into two rows.
Teams Paired; group can be any size.

Arrange the group into two rows, facing each other. Ask them to make eye contact with the person opposite. If there is an odd number of people, join in yourself. The object of the exercise is to 'hear' what the person opposite is 'saying' without using words. It is important that the main focus is the eyes, but general body language is useful too. Messages could range from 'What the hell am I doing here?' to 'What are you doing afterwards?' Tell participants to concentrate on hearing what the person opposite is saying to them – and not to forget to smile.

After 30 to 40 seconds rotate both groups in opposite directions for a count of five. Stop them facing a different person and repeat the exercise. Do this four or five times.

Feedback This is different from most ice-breakers in that it doesn't involve finding out facts. Instead, it works well at breaking down barriers. It is difficult to retain the initial barriers we erect around ourselves when really looking deeply into someone else's eyes. Tell the group this, after the exercise is complete.

Outcome As well as breaking down barriers, the exercise acts as a spur to people talking to one another. Try to allow time for introductions immediately afterwards.

Variations To create pairs rather than a full team you could restrict the exercise to a single pairing. This could be followed by a more traditional getting-to-know you exercise. With or without rotation, consider having brief verbal communication at the end of the non-verbal listening, in case curiosity makes participants frustrated. If the aim is general team building, it is possible to undertake this exercise with the whole group in a circle, picking someone opposite to communicate with, but people may be left out. To maximize the team spirit aspect, participants can put arms around their neighbours' shoulders, but this reduces the body language options.

Team building	✪✪✪
Ice-breaking	✪✪✪✪
Energy	✪✪
Creativity	✪
Fun	✪✪

3.9 True and false

Preparation None.
Running time 10 minutes.
Environment Whatever room you are meeting in.
Teams Individual; group can be any size that can sit around in a circle.

Each participant is given a couple of minutes to prepare. They need to have three 'facts' about themselves, two of which are false, one of which is true.

Go around the room allowing everyone to introduce themselves. They should say their name and then state the first fact. Then repeat their name and state the second fact. Finally, repeat their name and state the third fact. The rest of the team should decide for themselves which fact is true. Go round the room checking who believes what and then reveal the truth (a show of hands will do). Repeat this process for every participant. Each person should keep score of their hits and misses.

Finally, check the scores to see who is the most attuned to the group.

Feedback The repetition of name before each fact increases the memory of names far more than you would imagine. It is very easy to forget someone's name. It is hard to forget it when they tell you it three times in quick succession. We have found that stressing the need to make the true fact implausible increases the humour.

Outcome This introduction gives the names of the group to all of the members of the group in a way that increases the chance of remembering them. It also tags on a fact about that person.

Variations This can be run as a paired exercise with each member of the pair having to introduce their partner. If you do not introduce the true or false element at first, but ask them to find out a whole repertoire of surprising facts about their partner, then tell them to select the best and make up two lies, it increases the amount they know.

Team building	✪✪✪
Ice-breaking	✪✪✪✪
Energy	✪✪✪
Creativity	✪✪
Fun	✪✪✪

3.10 *I am and I know*

Preparation A ball (tennis ball, or similar size).
Running time 10 minutes.
Environment Room to stand in a circle.
Teams Individual. Group can be any size that can stand in a circle.

Start with the ball and say, 'I am <your name> and I know <the name of a famous person>'. Throw the ball to someone else in the circle and they must say, 'I am <their name> and I know…' but this time the famous person's first name must start with the last letter of the famous person's name that you used. For instance, 'I am Paul Birch and I know Margaret Thatcher' – throw the ball – 'I am Brian Clegg and I know **R**onald McDonald'.

If you cannot think of a name quickly enough to satisfy the group, you step out of the circle, passing the ball to your left. The next participant takes up where you failed. The last person in wins.

Feedback Bear in mind that those who are good at the exercise will have their names remembered more than those who are bad at it.

Outcome In general, people take away a few names from this, but it is played as much for fun as effectiveness.

Variations When someone drops out and the ball is passed on you can allow the person who picks up the ball to start from scratch with any name. This gives the opportunity for them to create some really tough challenges. If you are dealing with a group who already know one another you can use the exercise without the 'I am…' part. The linking letter can be also from first letter of surname to first letter of first name – eg from Michelle **P**feiffer to **P**aul Newman. A small variant if the exercise is proving too easy is that if someone gives a person with the first and last name starting with the same letter, the next player throws the ball back to them, rather than throwing it on to someone else. You can specify limits like real people or fictional characters.

Team building	✪✪
Ice-breaking	✪✪✪
Energy	✪✪✪✪
Creativity	✪✪
Fun	✪✪✪

3.11 Pairing hands

Preparation None.
Running time Three minutes.
Environment Room to stand in a circle.
Teams Individual; group can be any (even numbered) size.

This is a simple pairing-off exercise. Have the whole group stand in a circle and close their eyes. Then have them walk (or stumble) towards the centre of the circle with a hand held aloft. The other hand should be kept behind their back. Once squashed into the centre, with their eyes still closed, have them find someone else's hand, grip it and, as a pair, leave the melee.

Feedback It is often necessary to get a group split up into pairs to undertake breakout work and other exercises. Often this is done in a very unimaginative way. Pairing hands and the subsequent exercises 'Keys in the ring' (3.12) and 'String in the box' (3.13) are designed to make this more interesting. Pairing-off in this way may appear to be forced and somewhat laboured, but it removes the likelihood of cliques staying together, and adds some extra energy to subsequent activities.

Outcome This activity doesn't break the ice on its own but is a first step to a paired-off ice-breaker, or other pair-based exercise. However, as usual, close proximity (and the inevitable collisions) breaks down some barriers, and there is a buzz of energy after this quick exercise.

Variations Some participants are determined that they already know who their partner will be and so may keep their eyes open in order to force the choice. If you suspect that this will be the case you can just allow it to happen, you can blindfold all participants or you can pair off in sub-groups (ensuring that the pairs you don't want together are already in different groups). To increase disorientation, you can have everyone rotate on the spot several times before heading for the centre, or swap people's positions in the ring. In either case, it may be necessary to re-orient some of the participants before they continue.

Team building	✪✪
Ice-breaking	✪✪
Energy	✪✪✪
Creativity	✪
Fun	✪✪✪

3.12 Keys in the ring

Preparation None.
Running time Five minutes.
Environment Room to stand in a circle.
Teams Individual; group can be any (even numbered) size that can stand in a circle.

This is a simple pairing-off exercise. Have the whole group stand in a circle facing outwards. Number them one, two, one, two, etc so that everyone is assigned a one or a two. Have all of the number ones throw their car keys or house keys into the centre of the ring. Have the number twos pick up a set of keys at random. They then need to pair off with the owner of the keys.

Yes, you may have heard of this somewhere before. We are told that this was one of the pairing-off techniques used for partner-swapping parties. Since our invitations always got lost in the post, we never got a chance to use it there!

Feedback As always with anything to do with sex, mention of partner-swapping parties helps to oil the machine. Do make this explicit.

Outcome This activity has a limited ice-breaking effect on its own, but is better regarded as a first step to a paired-off activity. Like 'Pairing hands' (3.11) it causes considerable amusement, and there is extra activity involved in finding a match of keys to people, making the exercise take longer but making it even better for energy boosting.

Variations Rather than counting off ones and twos you could get people to select their own initial partners, without telling them why, then use the activity as a way of breaking up that pairing (one member of each pair throws in keys). Keys aren't the only option, though they have the best amusing connotation – any personal objects which can be specifically identified can be used, and you may need to widen the specification if someone present doesn't have a set of keys. You could have a few dummy sets of keys ready to help out.

Team building	✪✪
Ice-breaking	✪✪
Energy	✪✪✪
Creativity	✪
Fun	✪✪✪

3.13 *String in the box*

Preparation A box with strings coming out of it (see below).
Running time Five minutes.
Environment Room to sit in a circle.
Teams Individual; group can be any (even numbered) size.

This is a simple pairing-off game. This is an activity that is best used at the start of a session, as it makes it practical to have the string and the box waiting. You need half as many lengths of string as participants. The strings should stretch right across the circle with some room to spare. Drape the string across the room, over the box, allowing the surplus to drop into the box. Do not have one end of the string leave the box opposite the end that goes in. When the participants are sitting around the circle have them choose any end of string they fancy. When everyone has a piece of string they should reel in their partner.

Feedback The preparation is easier than it sounds, but this is a fair amount of work to generate pairs. It is worth the effort if you are doing a lot of pairing-off and want to use a different technique each time.

Outcome This activity doesn't break the ice a great deal on its own but it's a first step to a paired-off exercise. If you make a big deal of reeling in your partner you can raise energy levels slightly by getting people up and milling.

Variations To emphasize the reeling-in aspect, have half the participants sitting on chairs. The other half should be standing, and should follow the string as it pulls them, moving across the room until they hold hands with their catcher. To make this work, each string must have one end at a chair and one end away from a chair (though not opposite). With more preparation you can team people into larger groups by tying several lengths of string at the centre. You could deliberately confuse and add to the entertainment value by using different coloured strings tied in such a way that one end is not the same colour as the other.

Team building	✪✪
Ice-breaking	✪✪
Energy	✪✪✪
Creativity	✪
Fun	✪✪

3.14 *Trust me, I'll catch you*

Preparation None.
Running time Three minutes.
Environment Enough space for all the participants to stand in pairs.
Teams Pairs.

Each member of a pair takes it in turn to fall, being caught by their partner. The pairs should stand with one partner in front of the other. The front member of the pair should have their back to their partner. The person in front keeps their feet together and their arms by their side, while falling slowly backwards. Their partner catches them. They should start catching high (with little time to fall), and then lower a little. You must stress the danger of not catching. It could cause injury, and so has to be treated very seriously. Make sure that there is no possibility of anyone falling onto furniture or sharp objects. Make sure that you are appropriately insured before undertaking an exercise of this kind, and are aware of the responsibility you are undertaking.

Feedback It is very scary to fall backwards. If you don't trust your partner, it is almost impossible not to move your feet or spread your arms. We have never yet had anyone miss disastrously (although we have had a few pairs collapse into a messy, and usually giggling, heap). If there is time, have a short session getting feedback afterwards on how it felt to fall – and to catch.

Outcome As well as getting people moving, this is a very powerful demonstration of trust. There is inevitable team building and ice-breaking because of the closeness required between pairs.

Variations If you are confident enough in the team you can have pairs gradually falling further and further down. An ideal situation would be to operate this exercise with the mats used in soft play areas and with a good amount of space around each pair to minimize danger.

Team building	✪✪✪
Ice-breaking	✪✪✪
Energy	✪✪✪
Creativity	✪
Fun	✪✪

3.15 Sit on my lap

Preparation None.
Running time Two minutes.
Environment Enough space for all the participants to stand in a tight circle.
Teams Group activity; at least eight to 10 people.

Get the team to stand in a circle, each facing the back of the person beside them (in front of them). Then the whole team simultaneously lowers themselves into a sitting position and sits on the knees of the person behind them. Talk them through this, with a count-down and specific time to sit. Emphasize that it doesn't matter if they've done it before, it still has value.

Feedback Many people have seen or done this exercise before. For those who haven't it seems absurd that the group can all be sitting on its own laps and not collapse. For those that have it is still pretty amazing but they will tend to be fairly blasé about it.

Outcome This gets people up and about and is also a quick and effective demonstration of trust and interdependence. This exercise simply cannot work if even one person in the group doesn't trust themselves or the group enough to commit to it. If the initial result is to collapse in a heap, have a number of retries – don't give up straight away.

Variations A more advanced version of this activity is to have the whole group lean back on themselves. In fact, we've been told that it is possible to have everyone fall back into each other's arms but we haven't tried that because our public liability insurance isn't high enough. After a first go has proved it is possible, the exercise can be extended by putting everyone into the centre of the space, then asking them to repeat the exercise without any speech. If they are finding it difficult or impossible, point out that this does not mean no sound. If it is still failing, give them a minute to talk to each other first, then try without speech. This extension pushes up the creativity factor, making this a good all-round exercise.

Team building	✪✪✪
Ice-breaking	✪✪
Energy	✪✪✪✪
Creativity	✪
Fun	✪✪✪

3.16 Sense and sensibility

Preparation Half as many blindfolds as participants, coffee or tea break.
Running time Fifteen minutes.
Environment Space for movement.
Teams Pairs.

Needs an even number of people. Half the group are blindfolded, the other half are left without. Each blindfolded person is given another person as their minder. This exercise should take part across a coffee or tea break. The blindfolded person has to go through the usual activities they might undertake in such a break – getting a drink and a biscuit, going to the toilet, chatting with others, but under the guidance of the sighted person.

Feedback At the end of the break take five minutes to get feedback from the participants. How did the blindfolded people find these simple activities? Were the helpers helpful or a hindrance? What was unexpectedly difficult? How did the helpers feel?

Outcome By piggybacking on a natural break, this exercise can afford to take a little more time than is usual in this book. The exercise has a strong element of team building and ice-breaking. There is a mutual bond from the shared experience, and a forced interaction between blindfolded person and helper which will help break the ice. It also will generally inject energy and fun into a part of a meeting or training session which can be quite dangerous. Although breaks are essential, they can provide a negative distraction with participants tempted to telephone the office or sink into a near-somnolent state – this exercise makes sure this doesn't happen.

Variations You can stretch this exercise to fit the available opportunities. If you are involved in a residential session, it can be extended considerably. We have been involved in sessions where a whole evening was spent in blindfold/helper pairs, including time spent in the bar and a full evening meal. Whether this takes place in an open environment like a hotel or a closed conference centre, it can have a huge impact on the participants.

Team building	✪✪✪✪
Ice-breaking	✪✪✪✪
Energy	✪✪✪
Creativity	✪
Fun	✪✪✪

3.17 You're an animal

Preparation None essential, but timer or large clock and a noise maker are useful.
Running time Two minutes plus 30 seconds per participant.
Environment Enough open space for all participants to sit round.
Teams Group.

Give the participants two minutes to think of the animal which they think best represents them. They have to be able to say why, what special characteristics this implies, which other animal(s) they will get on with particularly well and which animals will be enemies. Then go round the group, giving each member a maximum of 30 seconds to put this across to the others.

Feedback This is largely a self-running exercise, but you will need to monitor the time strictly and be prepared to cut off an individual if they over-run. Probably the most effective way to do this is to have a loud noise maker (see Chapter 6) and sound it when the 30 seconds is up. You must also ensure that you get complete answers. Make it clear the time is still running if they don't give all the required information.

Outcome An effective ice-breaker which tells a little about the individuals involved, and how they see themselves, in a different and fun way.

Variations If group members can all be issued with water pistols and the room can take it (consider operating outside in good weather; fresh air is a natural energy booster), get them to soak those who over-run their 30 seconds. An interesting variation if you have the time is to have a third stage where the individuals get up from their seats and rearrange themselves so that they are near at least two other animals they are friendly with, and a minimum distance (say 2 metres) from all animals who they don't get on with. This both injects extra energy and ensures some listening during the descriptions rather than mentally practising their own information.

Team building	✪✪✪
Ice-breaking	✪✪✪✪
Energy	✪✪✪
Creativity	✪✪
Fun	✪✪✪

3.18 *You're great because...*

Preparation None.
Running time 10 minutes.
Environment No particular requirement.
Teams One or more, four to seven per team.

This is a strange ice-breaker because it requires participants to know each other to some degree already. Give them thinking time – they will need it. This is probably best done by announcing the intention of doing the exercise some time in advance.

In the exercise proper, each team member says to each other team member 'I think you are great because...', giving a single fact about them. It is very important this is done entirely sincerely. This should be made explicit, as it is very tempting to be humorous to cover embarrassment.

Feedback This exercise is particularly effective a few days after a new team has been brought together, or towards the end of a residential session. Team size is important – too small and it is too personal; too large and it lacks impact.

Outcome The exercise feels quite artificial and will involve considerable effort for those taking part. Saying nice things to other people's faces is always difficult, especially if you don't like them. This may require a considerable effort of will, but the outcome is a powerful strengthening of team spirit.

This exercise should only be used when the participants have a strong buy-in to the overall process. While it is very successful if undertaken seriously, it has been referred to as brainwashing when used on non-enthusiastic participants. Note that this doesn't mean the team members have to be enthusiastic about the technique – few will find it fun – but they do have to be positive about the session it forms a part of.

Variations With more time available you can increase the number of things said about each person to three. Don't try to go beyond this – it is impossible to go too far with someone you don't like. However, in most cases the participants will develop a camaraderie, even with the team members they did not get on well with before.

Team building	✪✪✪✪
Ice-breaking	✪✪✪✪
Energy	✪
Creativity	✪
Fun	✪

4

WARM-UPS

4.1 The paper-clip race

Preparation Twice as many paper-clips as people in the group.
Running time Five minutes.
Environment Enough space for all the participants to stand in two lines.
Teams Two equal teams; no limit to size.

Split the group into two. Get them to stand in two rows and give each person two paper-clips. The object of the race is to make a chain with the paper-clips as quickly as possible. The first person starts the chain, then passes it on to the next. As soon as the chain is completed it must be passed hand-to-hand back to the start of the row. At this point the whole team is to shout 'paper-clip' as loud as possible.

Feedback Be careful not to specify whether or not people can join their two paper-clips together before they receive the chain. If anyone asks, say you have explained all the rules. Make sure it's clear afterwards that anyone who thought that they had to wait for the chain to reach them before joining their two links was making a personal assumption – these are often a blockage to innovative thought.

Outcome The racing aspect gives this exercise considerable excitement. Help the teams to shout encouragement along the way. Standing up, moving around the room, engaging in physical dexterity are all helping to boost energy levels. Give the winning team a bag of sweets to share if you have one.

Variations Lots of possibilities here. Give each person more than two paper-clips. Once the chain is complete, it is passed back, being unclipped again as it goes. Instead of allocating paper-clips to individuals, give the team a big pile of clips and the task of matching in length (exactly) a chain you have made earlier and fixed on the wall. Perhaps most enjoyably, set the teams the task of making a long enough chain to entirely surround their team, with the chain joined to make a circle.

Team building	✪✪✪
Ice-breaking	✪✪
Energy	✪✪✪✪
Creativity	✪✪
Fun	✪✪✪

4.2 Balloon volleyball

Preparation A blown up balloon.
Running time Five to 10 minutes.
Environment Enough space for all the participants to stand either side of a row of tables.
Teams Two (roughly) equal teams; no limit to team size.

Unless your room already has a row of tables down the middle, first set the group the challenge of getting the room into this state with no guidance on how to do it. This provides an initial teamworking exercise. Split the group into two, putting the teams on either side of the row of tables. The teams knock the balloon across the tables. Each time the balloon hits the floor or the wall it counts as a point to the scoring team. Each team can only hit the balloon once, and it must cross the table. To start each play, hit the balloon down the middle of the row of tables from one end.

Feedback A pure warm-up, this one. It isn't essential to have a prize, but a bag of sweets for the winning team to share usually goes down well. As an even better alternative, produce one set of garish stickers with WINNER emblazoned on them and another with LOSER. This intentional pointing up of the trivial can cause considerable amusement – in fact the losers generally wear their stickers longer and more proudly than the winners.

Outcome Physical interaction and movement are the purposes of the game. Don't worry if people are rather cramped – getting in a tangle with each other is quite entertaining. This is a good fallback when a group is getting into a late afternoon slump.

Variations To get them moving even more you can change sides at half time. With larger groups, you may prefer to have several games going on at once – this way more people get a chance of contacting the balloon. If this is the case, still have the tables in a single continuous row, as overlaps add to the fun. If the room is cramped, consider taking this exercise into a more public space – extra energy is generated by the embarrassment factor.

Team building	✪✪✪
Ice-breaking	✪
Energy	✪✪✪✪
Creativity	✪✪
Fun	✪✪✪

4.3 The magic tunnel

Preparation A sheet of A4 (or letter) paper per team.
Running time Five minutes.
Environment Enough space for the teams to be well separated, or in breakout rooms.
Teams At least two teams; no more than five or six per team.

Split the group into teams of no more than five or six. Each team is given a sheet of paper. Their task is to pass the entire team through a hole in the sheet of paper. The hole must be surrounded by unbroken paper, and no other items are to be used. The first team to achieve this is the winner.

Feedback Point out the apparent impossibility on first approaching it. If one team got the idea, then others caught on to the general approach, note this. If no-one completes the exercise in five minutes, demonstrate the solution; if a team does, get them to show the rest what they did.

Solution. Fold the paper in two. Make a series of four tears, from the folded edge towards the other edge, leaving a clear centimetre of untorn paper in each case, as shown below.

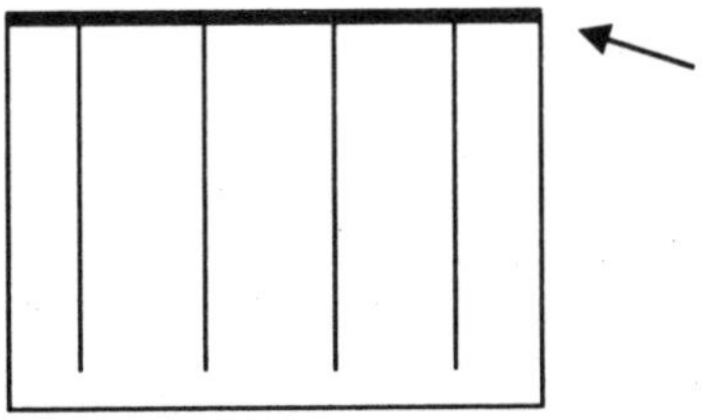

Make three tears in the opposite direction, between the original tears. Again, leave a clear centimetre at the end.

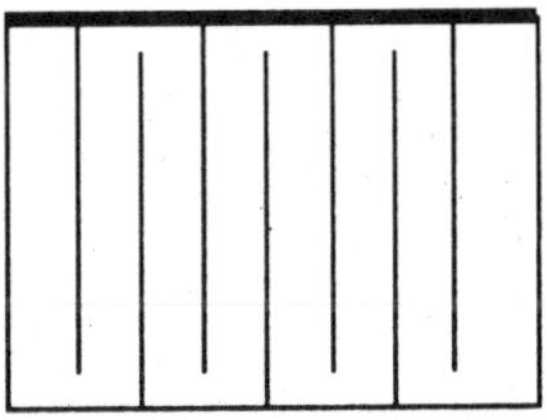

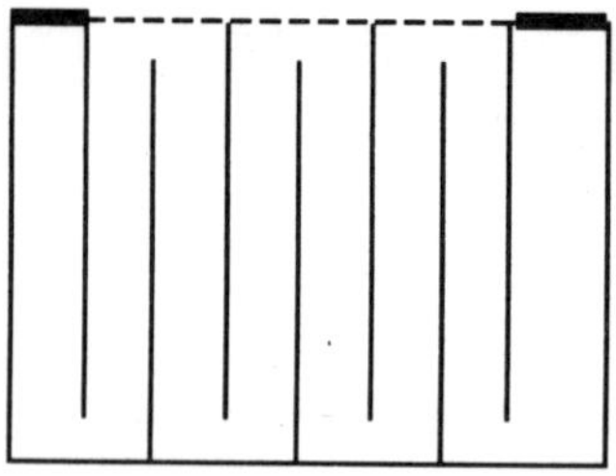

Tear along the crease of the three central creased end points. Open out the sheet of paper. It will make a paper ring, plenty big enough to pass a person through. Practise this before the event.

Outcome Provided the initial puzzle is solved there's a good physical aspect to getting the team members through the paper. The initial problem solving can be low energy, though, so this should be more a warm-up to get the group into a new frame of mind than to recover from low energy.

Variations If a team succeeds very quickly, give them a follow-up exercise with a quarter-sized piece of paper.

Team building	✪✪✪
Ice-breaking	✪
Energy	✪✪✪
Creativity	✪✪✪
Fun	✪✪✪

4.4 Bursting with energy

Preparation Lots of uninflated balloons (at least three per participant)
Running time Three minutes.
Environment Enough space for each team to stand together on open floor.
Teams At least two teams, ideally not more than seven or eight per team.

Split the group into teams. Each team should be given a set of (uninflated) balloons. There should be at least three balloons per person and preferably more. Without using any tools, the teams are to inflate their balloons and burst them. As each balloon bursts, the team shouts out the number of balloons burst so far by their team. The team with the most burst balloons in the time (or using up all their balloons first) wins.

Feedback Note that a team which decides not to inflate its balloons fully to save time may have found it harder to burst them. Find out how the teams went about organizing the tasks – did everyone blow and pop, or were tasks allocated? Find out any observations from this.

Outcome A huge energy booster, this one. There's lots of movement and physical activity, while most people find the act of popping a balloon slightly stressing, so there's extra nervous energy generated. Can be very noisy and exuberant – probably not a good idea to run this one in a quiet area.

Variations The choice between operating with two teams and several can make this exercise work quite differently in large groups. Each has benefits, but the usual advantages of keeping a group down to six or seven apply. An effective variation is to split the time available into blowing time and popping time: everyone tries both activities, and balloons have to be tied off, which adds to the confusion. The split time variation can be run two ways. Either you have a specific time for the changeover (say two minutes for blowing, one for popping) or, more interestingly, let the team decide when to switch, but once they have gone from blowing to popping, they can't go back.

Team building	✪✪
Ice-breaking	✪✪
Energy	✪✪✪✪
Creativity	✪✪
Fun	✪✪✪✪

4.5 On the square

Preparation One or two sheets of A4 (or letter) paper per team.
Running time Two minutes.
Environment Enough space for all the participants to be standing up in teams.
Teams At least two teams of at least six people; no upper limit.

Split the group into teams. Try for as few teams as possible, with up to about 30 people per team. Put the sheets of paper on the ground in front of the teams. For teams of up to five in size, use half an A4 (or letter) sheet for each team. Between 5 and 10 use a full sheet, and above 10 put appropriate numbers of sheets together. The object of the exercise is to get all members of the team standing on their sheet(s) of paper. No parts of the body can touch the ground or any other means of support other than the paper or other team members.

Feedback If the exercise proves too simple, get the team to halve the sheet size and try again. In fact, it is worth doing this anyway to make sure that there is a more dramatic challenge. On the square is a very quick exercise, so repeating it is not a problem.

Outcome Like all the best warm-ups, on the square gets people out of their seats, involved in physical interaction with one another and laughing. If the sheet is very small it can also prove an interesting challenge to work out how to get everyone on board.

Variations Generally this is best run as an exercise where everyone attempts to achieve the goal, but with even sized teams, it can be run as a first-to-complete exercise. As it can, in theory, be done with any sized group, it might be worth having a final extra session where everyone in the group, however large, attempts the exercise together.

Team building	✪✪✪
Ice-breaking	✪✪
Energy	✪✪✪✪
Creativity	✪✪
Fun	✪✪✪✪

4.6 Knots

Preparation None.
Running time Three minutes.
Environment Enough space to get the teams standing in unimpeded circles.
Teams Six, eight or 10 people in each team. Works best with a minimum of eight people. Will only work with an even number of people – the leader will need to be prepared to take part or stand back to even out the numbers.

Split the group into even numbered teams. The ideal number for a team is eight, but groups of six or 10 are entirely practical. Arrange the team, or teams, into a rough circle, facing inwards. Each member reaches into the circle and hold right hands with the person opposite. They should then hold the left hand of a different person. The team is now in a knot. The aim of the exercise is to untie the knot, leaving the team in a circle. In doing this they can rotate grips, but should not break the chain of hands.

Feedback This exercise is trivial with four people, mildly challenging with six, a little more with eight, downright difficult with 10 and verging on the impossible with 12. After that the combinatorial explosion means that, while it's technically soluble, it's practically impossible to get untangled.

Outcome Knots is an excellent warm-up that combines movement with a degree of practical thinking and team interaction (usually plenty of laughing and shouting involved). There is an element of ice-breaking too from the physical contact, and assisting each other through contortions, but concentration on the task in hand means that it has limited value in getting to know other team members.

Variations If there is time, demonstrate with larger and smaller groups how much easier or harder it gets. It is often difficult to undertake this exercise in a meeting room. We have found it effective to move the groups into a public space. This gives more room to manoeuvre, and also increases the warm-up potential by throwing in some exposure. If the group is particularly sluggish, you might consider taking them outside to do this exercise, freshening them up and countering the effect of air-conditioning.

Team building	✪✪✪
Ice-breaking	✪✪
Energy	✪✪✪✪
Creativity	✪✪
Fun	✪✪✪✪

4.7 Handcuffs

Preparation A string handcuff or a length of string per participant.
Running time Five minutes.
Environment Enough space to work in.
Teams Pairs.

String handcuffs consist of a length of string (at least 1 metre, preferably longer) with a loop tied at each end. The loop should be large enough to slip a hand in and out of easily. If you haven't prepared the loops in advance this can be the first stage.

Get the group into pairs with one handcuff per person – with an odd number you will have to take part. Ask one of each pair to slip both hands through the loops in their handcuffs. Ask the other member to slip a hand into one loop, then take the other end and pass it over their partner's handcuffs (between the handcuff and the body), finally slipping their remaining hand through. They are now linked. Their objective is to separate themselves without taking their hands out of their loops, or untying or cutting the string.

We have seen many ingenious solutions (cheating outrageously) but the 'correct' answer is to take the centre of your string through your partners wrist loop and over the back of their hand. Voila! You are free. You may find that you have actually tied a tighter knot at this stage. If so, reverse the process and then do it again in the opposite direction.

Feedback Very few people have come across this exercise but those that have must be asked to keep the solution to themselves. It works particularly well if you have played 'Knots' (4.6) beforehand, inducing a mindset that the solution involves untangling the people, rather than the string. Be sure to demonstrate the solution.

Outcome Touching and close contact are extremely effective at breaking down barriers. The outcome depends upon the participants' approach. Some treat it as a cerebral exercise and will stand thinking through the problem. Most leap straight in.

Variations The introductory element could be increased with an additional challenge. For instance, while separating yourselves, find out two things about your partner that will surprise everyone else.

Team building	✪✪
Ice-breaking	✪✪✪
Energy	✪✪✪
Creativity	✪✪✪✪
Fun	✪✪✪

4.8 Makeover

Preparation A selection of make-up, props, jewellery and costume items.
Running time 15 minutes.
Environment Ideally a separate area for each team, otherwise space to spread.
Teams At least three, with three to five people in each.

Divide the group into teams. You need at least three teams and at least three people per team. Otherwise only your resources limit numbers. Ask the teams to select a victim within the team that they will make up. To set the scene you can choose particularly overblown celebrities to make up in the style of, or you can leave it to the teams. The winning team is the one that has produced the most outrageous result in the time available.

Feedback This is a great warm-up for light hearted or barrier-breaking events. You must make sure that the set-up is entirely humorous and that it is clearly a joke that all team members are taking part in, or else you might find that you have a real victim in the group. You might also be prepared, as once happened to us, for the teams to rebel and use the facilitators as models.

Outcome There is a real element of competition but the subject matter makes it extremely light-hearted. The 'victim' is usually a volunteer and perversely, the more extreme the embarrassment factor, the more respected they become for volunteering. In fact, when building a team, making over the new team leader can be very positive.

Variations You can run this warm-up with no preparation and force the teams to rely on their own creativity to get hold of props, and use everyday items like paper-clips. The results are usually less outrageous but more challenging. If you are taking this approach, allow five minutes foraging time at the start, when team members can venture away from the meeting room to find items to use. There are circumstances, for example a residential course with many teams working simultaneously, where this exercise will benefit from having a camera to record the results, but only with the victims' permission.

Team building	✪✪✪
Ice-breaking	✪✪✪
Energy	✪✪✪
Creativity	✪✪
Fun	✪✪✪✪

4.9 Boy meets girl

Preparation None.
Running time Five minutes.
Environment Space to arrange the group into two parallel lines.
Teams Two, at least three people in each.

Arrange the group into two parallel lines. If there is an obvious team division, use it. The object of the exercise is for the two teams to tell a story with the title 'Boy meets girl'. The story progresses one word at a time, alternating from one team to the other, moving down the lines. One team should be attempting a happy ending, while the other team pushes for a depressing outcome.

If the total group is small you may need to have the story move up and down the line a few times (decide in advance). This is also the sort of exercise that improves with practice so you may want a trial run.

Feedback An exercise like this will not usually have winners and losers. When it works well it is because both sides are subverting the story of their opponents as it moves down the line. Declaring a winning team is essential if you are determined to have winners and losers, but do make clear that they are only just ahead (assuming that to be true). A better choice would be to give a small shareable prize to both teams.

Outcome This exercise varies greatly between being very high energy and low energy. When it works it is great fun and a source of laughter. When it doesn't take off it is a short diversion but little more. It isn't ideal for lifting a group from a very low energy state, as they need some impetus to get going. However, it is good to bring a middle-performing group up to top performance.

Variations Any story line can be used. It needs to be broad and open to a huge degree of interpretation. If you are dealing with a specific issue then the story could be concerning the outcome of that issue.

Team building	✪✪✪
Ice-breaking	✪
Energy	✪✪✪
Creativity	✪✪✪
Fun	✪✪✪

4.10 Steeplechase

Preparation A planned ride (see below).
Running time Five minutes.
Environment Space to arrange the group in a circle around the organizer.
Teams Individual; group can be any size.

Arrange the group in a circle around you and explain that you are going on a steeplechase. You might also say that what you are about to do is extremely silly, but for a very serious reason. As you race around the course you will pass certain obstacles; their job is to imitate your actions.

Get everyone crouching like a jockey in the saddle and start them patting their thighs to make a galloping sound. Then take them around a course. For example:

- a low branch – duck down and swish a hand over your head;
- hedge – jump over it, so sit up in the saddle and stop the hoof noises;
- left turn – lean in the saddle and pull the reigns over;
- right turn – lean in the saddle and pull the reigns over;
- trees to the left/right – swish a hand to the left/right of your head;
- 'oh look, there's an old man' – stop galloping, stroke an imaginary beard and 'hmmm' with disapproval at the horses (this comic interlude only works once);
- race for the finish line – spur the horses faster and faster until you pass the line.

Feedback The success of this warm-up depends largely on your chutzpah. Make sure the group understands the benefits of the energy it will inject – and that silliness is a positive part of it, but don't be overly defensive. In the unlikely event that it is not working after a minute or so, kill it and do something completely different.

Outcome This is a great warm-up for getting people up on their feet, involved in physical activity and laughing. It is difficult for anyone to stand aloof once the group as a whole gets going.

Variations The above are a small sample of possible obstacles. Throw in any you can think of, but do plan the course in advance – you must not be hesitant.

Team building	✪✪
Ice-breaking	✪
Energy	✪✪✪✪
Creativity	✪
Fun	✪✪✪✪

4.11 Circle of energy

Preparation None.
Running time Five minutes.
Environment Space to arrange the group into a circle.
Teams Individual; group can be any size that can stand in a circle.

Arrange the group into a circle. Explain that some people believe that everyone has energy flowing through their bodies, the Chinese call it chi, the Japanese call it ka. This circle is going to pass a ball of energy around.

Create an imaginary ball of energy in your hands and pass it on to the person on your left. Explain that anyone can add to or take from the energy as they see fit as they pass it around. When it has gone around the circle once, suggest that the next time you can get fancier by changing the shape or the consistency of the energy – it could be square, runny, sticky, etc. You might even decide to start throwing rather than passing it.

Next go around the circle passing on a hand clap, ie clap and pass this on. Try to get faster and faster. Next, pass on the clap and shout (anything loud and short). Finish with everyone continuing to clap as it passes them.

Feedback This exercise doesn't work as well with small groups so try it with at least eight or 10 people. If you have a smaller group that know one another already, they may be prepared to give it a go.

Outcome Considering that the activity involves standing in a circle it is surprisingly energizing and involving. The outcome is both raised energy levels and pulling people together into a group.

Variations There are a few variations included above. This started life as a tai chi exercise, simply passing a ball of chi. The additions have grown. What you add is limited only by your imagination. If you, or members of the group, are uncomfortable with the elements of Eastern philosophy then just make it an imaginary ball. You can still change its shape and consistency.

Team building	✪✪✪
Ice-breaking	✪✪
Energy	✪✪✪✪
Creativity	✪
Fun	✪✪

4.12 Beam me up

Preparation None.
Running time Five minutes.
Environment One chair per team of five and space to spread them.
Teams Five people per team.

Divide the group into teams of five people and ask them to select the largest member of the group to sit on the chair. The rest of the group stands around the chair, then each person entwines the fingers of both hands with the index fingers pointing straight out. They then place the index fingers under the knees and armpits of the person in the chair (one team member under one knee, one under the other, one under one armpit and one under the other). They should then attempt to lift the person using only these fingers. Most, or all groups will fail.

Now, get the group to raise their hands over the head of the person and to wave them around 'to absorb the energy of the person to be lifted'. This needs to go on for quite a while so that the arms tire slightly. Now quickly repeat the lifting exercise. Many or all of the groups will find it easy.

We don't know how this works. It is probably something to do with adrenaline or getting used to lifting the arms or something. You may want to try this out sometime ahead of using it in earnest to convince yourself that it will work.

Feedback This feels like magic when it goes well. The group are collectively convinced that what they are about to do will fail and despite this it proves easy.

Outcome There is a lot of laughter and some amazement generated by this. You will undoubtedly be asked for an explanation. Since we can't give you one you could make it up, claim ignorance or confess that it is a secret handed down through generations of your family that you have sworn never to divulge!

Variations There are variations you could play on the story or the set up of this warm-up but there's little you could do to alter the activity itself.

Team building	✪✪
Ice-breaking	✪✪
Energy	✪✪✪✪
Creativity	✪
Fun	✪✪✪

4.13 One spare square

Preparation A playing board per team (see below).
Running time 10 minutes.
Environment Room for teams to stand in a well-spaced line.
Teams Six or eight people per team.

This exercise needs teams of an even number of four or more, but six or eight works best. If you have an odd number of participants, join in yourself or use a waste paper basket as the final team member. Each team needs a playing board. This is a line of squares, one for each team member to stand in and one spare. The playing board could be carpet tiles, sheets of flip-chart paper or something created in advance.

The exercise starts with half the team at each end of the board (one per square). The two halves face each other, with the spare square in between them. The two halves take turns to move and they can only move into the spare square by stepping into it, if it is directly in front of them, or by 'jumping' someone facing them. They cannot jump more than one person. The objective of the game is to swap the two halves of the team.

Feedback Once a team has failed a few times, the exercise may appear impossible. Reassure them that it can be done. Try it a few times beforehand with small objects to get comfortable. You can give hints as the exercise progresses. A useful one is that you should never face someone's rear unless you are in the start or end position. Another is, never move away from someone facing the opposite way from you unless you are jumping. Don't give clues too soon.

Outcome This exercise has an unusually strong combination of physical movement and thinking. There might be some messages about communication come out of it, since team members will have different views of the solution.

Variations As an additional challenge, try combining two teams and solving it with twice as many people. The principle is the same, but the chance for error increases. To add energy, leapfrog the 'jumps', rather than going round each other.

Team building	✪✪✪
Ice-breaking	✪✪
Energy	✪✪✪✪
Creativity	✪✪✪
Fun	✪✪✪✪

4.14 The people machine

Preparation None.
Running time Five minutes.
Environment Room for the whole group to mill around.
Teams Individual; group can be any size that can stand in a circle.

Have the whole group stand in a circle and ask someone to step into the middle. You are going to build a machine, with each person becoming a component part. The person in the centre is the first element of the machine. To do this they will move oddly and make a noise (eg flail their arms around and clank or squeak). One by one the rest of the group follows on behind them each adding their own (different) movement and their own (different) noise. Each person should be connected to at least one other, though the connection can be remote (for example, one hand following the movement of someone else's foot) or more physical.

Feedback Make sure that the participants do not feel constrained by the circle; they should move around as much as takes their fancy. With one particularly loud group we moved out of our meeting room into the hotel lobby, to great effect.

Outcome This sounds silly and somewhat trivial. It is, but it is none the worse for it. The exercise is great fun and works well as a start to bonding people together. If you need an activity that increases the energy and the laughter of a group, this is a great one.

Variations If the group is not being particularly imaginative, you can pre-assign movements and noises to some of the later components. A very effective variation is to get the machine moving in a circle when everyone is in place and, at a signal from you, to have everyone take over the characteristics of the person in front of them (their movements and noises). Another small variant is to insist everyone connects to at least two others.

Team building	✪✪✪
Ice-breaking	✪
Energy	✪✪✪✪
Creativity	✪
Fun	✪✪✪✪

4.15 Elastic band race

Preparation A large elastic loop for each team.
Running time Five to10 minutes.
Environment Room to split into teams and still have space.
Teams Four to 20 people per team.

Divide into teams with no fewer than four people in a team. If your teams are larger than 20 people you may want to consider splitting further.

Give each team a large elastic band. This can be made from elasticated cord or bungee rubber if necessary. The size should be such that it will stretch around any team member yet still be a tight fit. The object of the game is for every team member to pass through the elastic band. The first team to achieve this wins.

Feedback As with all of the competitive activities, the element of competition adds zest that is difficult to achieve any other way. Make sure there is a lot of cheering on by fellow team members – you might have to cheerlead this to get it going. Small prizes, stickers and the like go down well with an exercise like this, especially if there is something for everyone.

Outcome This is a high energy activity and, if the band is difficult enough to get through, can be hilarious.

Variations It is possible to allow or disallow help from other team members. We have generally found it better to leave everyone to their own devices as the exercise can become trivial given enough help. If you have a little more time, have one round allowing assistance, then another without, which will emphasize the difference. With slightly larger bands, you can run a variant requiring the team to pass through the band in pairs (check that this is practical with your bands first). If using this variant it is best to select the pairs randomly (see exercises 3.11 to 3.13 for some ways of pairing up) to avoid anyone being left out.

Team building	✪✪✪
Ice-breaking	✪✪
Energy	✪✪✪✪
Creativity	✪
Fun	✪✪✪✪

4.16 Sheepdog trials

Preparation A blindfold for each participant.
Running time 10 to 15 minutes.
Environment Space to move around for long distances, ideally outdoors.
Teams Two teams, any size.

Divide the group into two teams. The objective of the warm-up is for a shepherd to guide his or her flock of sheep into a pen.

The control of the sheep must be through whistles or nonsense words (such as 'come by') and not through commands of left or right, etc. Give each team time to establish their signals. The teams choose one team member as a shepherd. A pen should be set up by the shepherds – this needn't be sophisticated. The sheep (the remaining team members) are taken some distance away and put on blindfolds. The shepherds then guide the sheep into the pen.

Feedback This activity relies on having lots of space – usually available (and wasted) outdoors. It would be possible to run in a large hall but we haven't tried it. It also provides harmless amusement for the staff or other users of the same venue.

Outcome Aside from the fun there are a lot of lessons about the value of thorough preparation in this activity. It can be particularly instructive if one team takes significantly longer than another.

Variations You can run both teams at the same time or separately (as a time trial). Running them together provides more amusement through confused commands and collisions. You can allow the sheep to hold onto one another. This makes the activity significantly easier. If you are not allowing this then it pays to warn the shepherd that they will need to be able to give commands to individual sheep and must therefore name them (but should not use their real names). Controlling the sheep separately adds significantly to the time taken. An alternative with large groups is to have two to four players without blindfolds. These are dogs, who move only on command. The sheep now ignore commands and simply mill around, or move away from taps or barks issued by the dogs.

Team building	✪✪✪
Ice-breaking	✪✪
Energy	✪✪✪✪
Creativity	✪✪
Fun	✪✪✪✪

4.17 Magic carpet

Preparation A rug or strong length of fabric for each team (large enough for the whole team to stand on).
Running time 10 minutes.
Environment Open space on a polished floor.
Teams Two to six people per team.

The object of this activity is for teams to race, on carpets, across a room. There must be clear start and end points. Divide the group into teams and give each team a rug (make it a very cheap one because it may well be destroyed). Teams larger than six people will find this activity very hard, so keep teams small.

The teams must stay on their rug and move the rug across the room. They can do this in any way that works for them but no part of their bodies may touch the ground off the rug.

Feedback It is unlikely that you will run this warm-up without a rug being torn or one of the team members falling from the rug. You must establish in advance whether there is a sanction for this (such as returning to the start) other than the delay caused by reorganizing the team. No prizes are necessary in an exercise like this. The most effective way we have seen is to have one or more team members at the front holding the leading edge of the rug and for all team members to jump simultaneously. Those at the front pull the rug forward as they all jump. It is also possible to move the rug by sliding it rather than jumping.

Outcome This is a very physical exercise which is great for raising energy levels. It can forge small teams but, like any team activity, can also create minor conflicts when mistakes occur.

Variations If you only have one rug, you can time each team across the room. This is less effective than a straight race as later teams are able to watch the technique of earlier ones and also because the need to stand around waiting lowers energy.

Team building	✪✪✪
Ice-breaking	✪✪
Energy	✪✪✪✪
Creativity	✪✪
Fun	✪✪✪✪

4.18 Balloon racing

Preparation One or two balloons for each person in the group.
Running time Three minutes (may take longer with a large group).
Environment Enough space for all the participants to line up. If there is a very large group you can run heats and so get away with less space.
Teams Individual.

Stand the group in a line, each armed with a balloon that is in some way unique (colour or has their name on it). The participants blow up the balloons and release them. The balloon that travels furthest down the room wins. If you wish you can allow two balloons per person to allow them to perfect their technique.

Feedback This type of activity is simply a diversion. Make sure the participants are aware that this is undertaken for a reason – to produce the outcomes below – or it may be difficult to get them away from what they are doing to take part in a silly game. Small prizes go down well, but are not essential in this exercise.

Outcome Like all activities with a party game feel, this exercise produces laughter and raises energy levels. There is more to this fun activity than increasing energy levels, though. It is very effective at switching people away from their current focus, giving them a chance to come at a problem from a different direction or preparing them for addressing something completely different.

Variations This activity can be run as a team exercise with either the furthest individual travel or the sum of the distances determining the winner. If a long room is available it is possible to allow several goes with the same balloon (increasing the physical activity as the participants run down the room). It is also possible to run the exercise as a race to get the balloon across a line, which requires multiple 'shots' from the point where the balloon lands.

Team building	✪✪
Ice-breaking	✪
Energy	✪✪✪
Creativity	✪
Fun	✪✪✪✪

4.19 Out for the count

Preparation None.
Running time Two minutes.
Environment Enough open space for all participants to stand up, ideally in a circle.
Teams Individual; no restrictions.

Get everyone standing up, in a circle if space permits. Start everyone clapping in rhythm. This should be reasonably quick, around two claps per second. Once the clapping is well established, get everyone to count loudly together. Each number should coincide with the clap. Get them to run from one to 10, then back down from 10 to one. Do this twice. You will need to talk between runs to organize them – give them a bit of warning along the lines of 'okay, here we go, from one to 10 then back down from 10 to one, and... (two claps) one, two...'. Once they are feeling confident get them to do the same in French (again, have two goes).

Feedback Groups will get along reasonably well until it comes to counting backwards in French. As most people learn foreign numbers in sequence, counting backwards is much harder, resulting in chaos.

Outcome The exercise gets them out of their seats and active. When everything goes wrong on the French, there is usually considerable laughter. A big plus for this one is it's very quick, there is no preparation and it can use any room configuration.

Variations To make the exercise a little longer (and generate more hilarity), after running the exercise, tell them this is an old choirmaster's technique. In Anglican chant, psalms are sung in two groups of 10 notes, so choirs often learn the chant by singing one to 10, then 10 to one. As they were so good the first time (it doesn't matter whether they were or not) you are going to repeat it, but sing the numbers. Do it exactly as before but sing up a scale as the numbers go up, and down as the numbers come down. Give them the starting note as you finish the introduction – make sure this is low enough to be able to sing nine higher notes after it.

Team building	✪
Ice-breaking	✪✪
Energy	✪✪✪
Creativity	✪
Fun	✪✪✪✪

4.20 Cow tails

Preparation One large picture of a cow, one blindfold, and one tail with sticky fixer per team.
Running time Five minutes.
Environment Enough room for one member of each team to wander about and to have a cow per team fixed to the wall.
Teams At least two, but better with four or more teams. No team size restriction.

Blindfold one member of each team and give them a tail. Each team has a specific cow on the wall. Their task is to guide their blindfold member to their cow and get the tail stuck in the right place. They can only communicate with the blindfold team member by mooing. Before starting, give the teams one minute to arrange a system to use moos to steer the blindfold person. Then position the blindfold people well away from their cows. Stop the exercise after four more minutes if all the tails aren't in place.

Feedback The basic task is non-trivial, but many teams don't give enough consideration to dealing with interference from other teams' mooing. There are interesting parallels in inter-team communication. Have some appropriate prize for the winning team (and perhaps a booby prize for the worst result).

Outcome There's lots of energy here (make sure the whole team are on their feet), once the participants overcome feeling silly about going 'moo'. There is also the opportunity to be creative in the way moos are used to co-operate (and possibly also in disaster recovery, if cross-moos are confusing the issue).

Variations We have used a cow to distance the exercise from the traditional party game of pinning the tail on the donkey, and because 'moo' is a satisfyingly silly noise to make. As a variant you could choose another animal or something completely different to suit the audience (dock the shuttle on the space station, get the sausage in the bun…) provided you can come up with an appropriate sound to use as instruction. It is possible to use a single cow as the target for all teams, maximizing collisions and confusion.

Team building	✪✪
Ice-breaking	✪✪
Energy	✪✪✪
Creativity	✪✪
Fun	✪✪✪✪

4.21 Peer groups

Preparation None.
Running time Five minutes.
Environment Enough room for all group members to mingle.
Teams Group activity.

Get the entire group standing up. Tell them you would like them to get together in teams whose surnames start with the same letter (with a smaller group, make this surnames A to C, etc as appropriate – you will need to prepare this ahead of time). If they haven't achieved this after two minutes, stop them anyway. Now you want them teamed up with people who drive the same make of car. After a minute or so, stop them again. Now you want them together with people with the same colour of underwear. After a minute or so, return them to their seats.

Feedback Allow more time for the first session, because with practice it becomes easier to get together with similar people. To start with there will be some tentative asking others, until someone takes the initiative and stands on a table (or equivalent), shouting their selection at the top of their voice. An excellent aspect of this particular exercise is that the bigger the numbers are, the better. We have used it with several hundred people to great effect.

Outcome Almost a pure energizer, this is an excellent exercise to pull out of the bag at a moment's notice to revive a flagging group or to get them into the frame of mind for concentration. We have used it very effectively with a group that had spent most of the afternoon being lectured, when we wanted some positive contribution from them.

Variations You can use almost anything to group people, though ideally it should have a relatively small number of options (age, for instance is too broad). Colour of underwear is a great finisher, because it has a slight frisson of naughtiness, leaving the participants on an energetic high. Don't be tempted to replace it with something more tame, whatever the audience. If you want an alternative finisher, make sure it has a similar connotation (eg what you wear in bed).

Team building	✪
Ice-breaking	✪✪
Energy	✪✪✪✪
Creativity	✪✪
Fun	✪✪✪✪

4.22 Giants, witches and dwarves

Preparation None.
Running time Five to 10 minutes.
Environment Space enough for the group to stand in two lines (possibly space enough to run around as well).
Teams Two, more than six people in total (we've used this warm-up with over 200).

Divide the group into two teams, in lines facing each other. Explain the rules. Giants, witches and dwarves is a team version of paper, scissors and stones. Giants defeat witches by beating them on the head. Witches defeat dwarves by casting spells on them. Dwarves defeat giants by beating the knees out from beneath them. If a team decide to be giants they must all wave their fists above their heads and roar at the tops of their voices. If the team decide to be witches they must throw spells and cackle in a really loud voice. If the team decide to be dwarves they must drop to their knees and beat the knees out from under the giants whilst shouting 'Ni, ni, ni, ni'. Demonstrate these moves with over-the-top acting.

Give the team time to decide how they will all do the same thing at the same time. Any team with more than one type loses. Play the best of three or five. Between rounds everyone remains in earshot of the other team, so tactics can't be discussed explicitly.

Feedback There are messages about planning and communication that can be extracted. We have never used this activity without one of the teams either deciding that they need not plan, they'll play it by ear or going for an over elaborate method of cueing the next round.

Outcome This is a high-energy game which changes the mood of a group swiftly.

Variations You can change the rules and have the winning team chase and capture one (or more) of the losing team. This is much more active but is also riskier. You will need to ensure that the room makes this practical without participants damaging it, its contents or each other.

Team building	✪✪✪
Ice-breaking	✪✪
Energy	✪✪✪✪
Creativity	✪✪
Fun	✪✪✪✪

4.23 Suck and blow

Preparation A business card, a playing card, a beer mat or similar (more than one if you are racing).
Running time Five minutes.
Environment Room to stand in a circle or into a number of lines if you are racing.
Teams Whole group or teams of any reasonable size.

It is a sad reflection on the world that we should think twice before including an exercise that has been effective for many years because of the fear of AIDS, herpes and other diseases transmitted by bodily fluids. Still, for what it's worth, here it is. Note the variants below to get round this problem.

Get the entire group standing in a circle with their hands behind their backs. The object of the game is that one person sucks the card onto his or her mouth and passes it to the next person. They in turn pass it on until the item has travelled around the circle.

Feedback This exercise originates as a great party game and works well as an energizer with people who know one another. It may be a little intrusive for some so use with caution.

Outcome Lots of laughter and a raising of energy. Considerable ice-breaking too, if there is already a broad familiarity.

Variations Instead of standing in a circle, have teams line up. Each team then races to pass a card from one end of the line to the other. If there is any concern about health, it is possible to fall back on the alternative of passing balloons, balls or fruit from person to person using the elbows, knees or head and shoulder to grip the item. Make sure it is physically possible to do before using the specific item/bodily part combination. Knees and head/shoulder combinations are more intimate than elbows, so result in better ice-breaking, but are also more likely to cause discomfort if the participants don't know each other.

Team building	✪✪
Ice-breaking	✪✪✪
Energy	✪✪✪
Creativity	✪
Fun	✪✪✪✪

4.24 Magnet race

Preparation A few strong, cylindrical magnets.
Running time Five minutes.
Environment A room with a magnetic whiteboard (as large as possible).
Teams Individual or small teams.

Ideally the magnets you use for this should be marked with coloured spots and each person should be assigned a colour.

If they are strong enough, round magnets will roll down a magnetic white board without leaving the surface until they reach the bottom. The object of this activity is to hold races to see who can cause their magnet to travel furthest across the room after it has rolled down the whiteboard. If a magnet leaves the board before a pre-defined point, it doesn't count.

Feedback This seems a rather silly aside from the real business of the day but lightens the mood and takes the mind off whatever activity is under focus, giving an opportunity to come at it afresh. It is worth explaining this, or the activity may seem too frivolous.

Outcome Principally this activity provides diversion, some laughter and a chance to have some fun. If run in small teams it can engender team spirit, particularly in some of the variations described below.

Variations This can be run as a team game or an individual game. If it is run in teams, each team member should have a chance to roll and the furthest roll counted. If this is not done it is very disengaging for those not rolling. With more resources, a more impressive version can be achieved by racing the tumbling plastic insects with sticky feet – these roll down windows, whiteboards, or smooth walls. Given significant time (for example on a residential course) this can be developed into a major event with tracks, etc. If appropriate magnets (or tumbling insects) can't be found, get hold of a sloping surface (tip a table, unscrew a whiteboard from a wall) and use this to race balls down and across the floor.

Team building	✪✪
Ice-breaking	✪
Energy	✪✪✪
Creativity	✪
Fun	✪✪✪✪

5

TIME-OUTS

5.1 Towering

Preparation Roll of brown paper or newspaper and roll of sticky tape per team.
Running time Five minutes.
Environment Enough space to work in.
Teams Two or more teams, three or four people per team.

The group is split into teams of three or four people. This exercise will only work with two or more teams. The teams are given the challenge to build the tallest free-standing tower they can, using only the paper and tape you give them. At the end of the time period, the towers must be totally unsupported.

Feedback There may not be an outright winner, as the ceiling could limit height, but be prepared to choose a winner on a combination of height and artistic appeal – or several winners. If any of the towers look particularly flimsy, try blowing them to see if they fall over – this will amuse the other teams – but still count them as successful. The exercise benefits from silly prizes, eg small bag of sweets.

Outcome The tower building exercise gets the team working together, but the primary aim is to get the individuals involved doing something completely different from the task in hand to increase creativity.

Variations You should allow teams with the insight to do so to move to a different part of the room or into the corridor if this gives a greater ceiling height. Taking this exercise outside can be interesting (especially with light winds). Given longer, the exercise can be specifically to build the most attractive tower at least 2 (or 3) metres in height. This would allow for some artistic input with whiteboard pens, and more consideration of the form of the tower, rather than its height. Various alternative materials can be used. Try wallpaper lining paper or photocopier paper. Can be run with no means of joining the paper, or only paper-clips, but allow the teams a little longer in this case.

Team building	✪✪✪✪
Ice-breaking	✪✪
Energy	✪✪✪
Creativity	✪✪✪
Fun	✪✪✪✪

5.2 Ands

Preparation None.
Running time Three minutes.
Environment No special requirements.
Teams Two or three people per team.

Split the group into small teams. The challenge is to be the first team to be able to tell a (very) short story in which the word 'and' appears five times in a row, yet the story still makes sense. As soon as a team has a possible solution, they should alert the organizer. The other teams should be put on hold while the story is told.

Feedback Early attempts may well stretch the rules considerably. Be positive about them, but allow the other teams to continue, finding alternative solutions. If none of the teams has a result in five minutes, award the best attempt with a prize. Make sure you are able to provide a valid solution if one has not been reached. A simple example is as follows: Smith and Jones, the butchers, want a new shop sign. It comes back from the sign writers with the words poorly spaced. Smith calls the sign writer and says, 'This is no good. I want the spaces between Smith and "and" and "and" and Jones to be the same.'

Outcome This is not an exercise that will inject a huge amount of energy, so it is best applied when the group already has plenty of enthusiasm, but you need a change of direction. The requirement to think laterally is a good preparation for creative work. You can artificially add a small energizer by requiring the teams to stand in different parts of the room while they work on their solutions, rather than sitting round a table.

Variations If the solution is reached too quickly (or you want to show off to the group), set the challenge of increasing the 'and' count to seven. This requires a slightly broader interpretation of the rules. Now the sign writer is producing a sign for a charity walk. Again the spacing is faulty. 'I want the spaces between Northumberland and "and" and "and" and Andover to be the same.'

Team building	✪
Ice-breaking	✪✪
Energy	✪✪
Creativity	✪✪✪✪
Fun	✪✪✪

5.3 Tongue twisters

Preparation None.
Running time Five minutes.
Environment No special requirements.
Teams Two to four teams with at least two people per team.

Split the group into teams. There should be no more than four teams (unless you want to spend more than five minutes on the exercise), but each team must have at least two people. The teams are then given three minutes to devise the best original tongue twister they can. In the rest of the time, each team tries out their tongue twister on the next team in order. The target team is to stand up and repeat the tongue twister three times, as quickly as possible. The team judged to have produced the most effective tongue twister wins a prize (if available).

Feedback Comment on what makes a good tongue twister after the exercise: repetition and rapid changes of mouth part positions between similar words. A good illustration to help them see what is happening is 'cricket, critic, wicket'. Get everyone to repeat it several times quickly while concentrating on what is happening physically in his or her mouth.

Outcome This is a good energy builder, as there is usually plenty of laughter, both in the teams when devising the tongue twister and when the teams are in competition. There is a creative stimulus from the need to analyse what makes a good tongue twister, something few people have thought about.

Variations Few variations are required here, but alternatives in the section when the tongue twisters are being tried out are for all the team to speak the tongue twister, all members of every other team to speak it, or just one person from the next team to speak it. With small numbers, all members of every team would be best. With very large numbers its probably best to keep it to an individual or the results will be too blurred.

Team building	✪✪✪
Ice-breaking	✪✪
Energy	✪✪✪
Creativity	✪✪✪
Fun	✪✪✪✪

5.4 Buy me

Preparation None.
Running time 10 minutes.
Environment No special requirements.
Teams Maximum of 10 people in total.

Send out the group as individuals to find an object somewhere in the location other than the meeting/event room. They have to bring something back within two minutes. It should be something interesting, which they aren't going to get into too much trouble for moving. When everyone has returned, each person has 30 seconds to sell their object: to describe why the organizer should spend his or her money on it. The person who sells their item best wins a prize. Ideally no more than seven or eight people should be involved, as it gets boring if too many objects are covered. Allow a minute at the end for returning objects.

Feedback React to enthusiasm and humour in the sales technique. Keep the process tight.

Outcome The process of going out and getting the objects is a good energy generator. It is possible to lose energy during the selling stage, as at any one time most of the team are not active, hence the need to keep the process tight. It helps to have each salesperson stand up, and to encourage the audience to comment. However, the prime benefit of this exercise is as a change of direction. Encourage the participants to bear their object and their sales talk in mind when they return to the subject of the session – it might lead to some very original thinking.

Variations If conditions don't permit it, you can get people to sell objects they have about their person, though this removes the considerable advantages of getting them moving out of the room. A variant which can be very effective is to get each team member to sell a piece of their clothing, which they must remove before sale. Ideally give them the opportunity to leave the room to remove it – you may get some more daring items that way, and the more daring, the more effective as a stimulus.

Team building	✪
Ice-breaking	✪✪
Energy	✪✪✪
Creativity	✪✪✪✪
Fun	✪✪✪✪

5.5 Blindfold birthday

Preparation Blindfolds (not essential – see variations).
Running time Five to 10 minutes.
Environment Enough space for teams to line up and mill around a little.
Teams At least five people per team.

Split the group into teams, ideally with at least five people per team. Their task is to get into a line in order of their birthdays. The problem is, they have to do it blindfolded, without speaking. Give the teams two minutes to discuss tactics (with the promise not to mention their birthdays). At this point the blindfolds go on. Mix the order of the individuals within each team, in case of collusion. Now there is silence for three minutes while they attempt to get in the right order. If they feel they are in the right order, they should indicate it by all holding their hands in the air. Note the possible winner, but don't stop the rest until the time is up.

Feedback Remember to check the birthdays – they may not have it right. Spend a minute getting a feel for the tactics used – see if the approach varies from team to team.

Outcome There is a good combination of creative thinking and energy in this exercise. Being blindfolded makes the participants more aware of other senses, and can result in some interesting interaction, giving a degree of ice-breaking too.

Variations If there is time, a good way of making this an even more effective time-out is to have an initial five-minute session when each team makes blindfolds for another. This also means the exercise can be performed without preparation, apart from having the materials available. We have found that items typical to a meeting room – a sheet of flip-chart paper, sticky tape and whiteboard pens – can produce some very creative blindfolds. The exercise has been attempted without the initial tactics talk, but it can be very frustrating for those taking part and is not recommended.

Team building	✪✪✪
Ice-breaking	✪✪✪
Energy	✪✪✪✪
Creativity	✪✪✪✪
Fun	✪✪✪

5.6 Animals

Preparation Four sheets of flip-chart paper.
Running time Six minutes.
Environment At least two tables (preferably four) and room for the group to move around them.
Teams At least four people in total.

Split the group into four teams, as equal in size as possible, though it isn't essential. Put four sheets of flip-chart paper out on tables. If there is time, draw three horizontal lines on each sheet, dividing them into quarters. Each team draws an animal's head on the top quarter, then folds over the top of the sheet, leaving only the lines at the end of the neck showing. Allow them a strict 45 seconds before moving on. The teams move round to the next table, and contribute the upper body. Another move and the lower body, another move and the legs/tail. The teams now return to their original sheet, open it out, stick it on the wall and spend one minute deciding what the animal is and why it is significant to their team. Each team then gives a 30-second presentation on their animal to the other teams.

Feedback Make some observations on both the animals and the description. There doesn't have to be a prize for this one – if there is, give it for the most outrageous or hilarious description.

Outcome This is a good, general-purpose time-out. The movement from table to table and the tight timing keeps the energy up, while coming up with animal parts and particularly with a justification for the resultant mongrel stimulates the creativity. Humour is liable to arise both from the description and the (lack of) quality of the drawings.

Variations The subject to be drawn can be a person, but the result is less flexible. It's important not to drop the description phase, as this is where most creativity comes in, and without it the exercise falls rather flat. If numbers are appropriate, institute a rule that a different person must draw each part, to maximize the direct input of each individual.

Team building	✪✪
Ice-breaking	✪✪
Energy	✪✪✪
Creativity	✪✪✪✪
Fun	✪✪✪

5.7 Ideas to get you fired

Preparation A flip-chart or pad per team.
Running time 10 minutes.
Environment Room to split the group into a number of teams.
Teams At least two, no more than five people per team.

Split the group into teams, ideally with three to five people each. Isolate the teams by using breakout rooms, or separating them as much as is possible in a single room. Each team spends five minutes brainstorming 'ideas to get you fired'. Encourage the teams to be wild and original. The teams should generate as many ideas as possible, each being a possible reason to lose your job. After generating ideas, the team should spend a minute choosing the idea they'd most like to put into action. Get the groups back together. Each team then has a minute to describe their favourite idea to the others. The other teams should come up with ways of making the idea practical.

Feedback When the teams come back together, forbid negative comment – only allow positive suggestions. This may involve modifying the idea, for example an idea involving killing someone (impractical) can be modified to finding a way to get them out of their job or into another job.

Outcome This exercise is about enhancing creativity. By looking at anti-establishment ideas, the participants will break the constraints limiting their innovation. The result will be lots of impossible ideas, but even if they remain such, the participants will be in a freer frame of mind, and it is quite possible that an effective idea will be generated. This isn't the objective, but it may be an outcome.

Variations You often get more originality by having each member of the team generate ideas individually, then pooling their thinking, but this requires an extra five minutes. You can choose five ideas rather than a single one to carry forward, but again this takes longer. If possible, get the flip-charts from the sessions and put them around the area where the participants take a break. The more public the area, the better.

Team building	✪✪✪
Ice-breaking	✪
Energy	✪✪
Creativity	✪✪✪✪
Fun	✪✪✪✪

5.8 A to Z

Preparation At least three flip-charts or whiteboards. At least one different coloured pen for each team.
Running time Five minutes.
Environment Meeting/training room.
Teams Minimum two teams, not bigger than five or six people in each.

Split the group into teams. Each team should be assigned a colour, and either be given a pen per team, or have a full set of (working) pens for each team colour at each flip-chart or whiteboard. Position the flip-charts and whiteboards around the room. At the top of each, write a subject. It might be film titles, animals, cities and pop stars. The teams then have three minutes to write up examples of the heading on the appropriate boards. Each team can only use its own pen. Each board can only have one entry beginning with a particular letter (with a subject like pop stars, you should specify which name).

Feedback When the time is up, get the teams away from the boards as quickly as possible (they may be tempted to keep writing). Get them to add up their own team's score. Lead them briefly through the contents of the boards, pointing out any silly, interesting or downright wrong entries.

Outcome Although this time-out involves an element of standing and thinking, the need to move around the different boards, and the need to make use of a letter before anyone else does gives energy too. Coming up with lists in this way can be surprisingly effective as a way of stimulating thought and moving away from the conventional. Make sure that none of the topics bear any relation to the subject at hand.

Variations It's probably best to stick to a subject you know a little about, as you may be called on to referee. Other topics might be: household objects, rivers, countries, historical characters, fictional characters, book titles, artists and so on. With a little more preparation time, write the letters A to Z on each board, making it easier to ensure that there is only one of each letter on each board.

Team building	✪✪
Ice-breaking	✪
Energy	✪✪✪
Creativity	✪✪✪✪
Fun	✪✪✪

5.9 *Plane sailing*

Preparation An A4 (or letter) sheet per participant.
Running time Five minutes.
Environment Normal meeting or training room.
Teams At least two teams, preferably not bigger than five or six people in each.

Split the group into teams. Each team is given a sheet of paper for each team member. They then have three minutes in which each member of the team makes a paper plane. During the three minutes, they also have to decide which plane is to represent their team, without trying the planes out. At the end of the three minutes, the elected team members line up and send off their paper planes. The winner (with the plane that flies farthest) gets a small prize. Something appropriate like a cheap toy plane goes down well.

Feedback It is quite possible that each team has several planes which might be winners. One of the lessons of this exercise is that there isn't a single right answer to a problem – but you have to become comfortable with choosing an option and getting on with it, rather than continuing to dither over the possible outcomes.

Outcome This isn't a particularly high energy time-out, but it is an excellent one for getting the participants away from their current train of thought and putting them onto new directions. Choosing a plane to represent the team without seeing them fly is an important part of the exercise, both to emphasize the possibility of more than one right answer and to point out the risk inherent in many decisions.

Variations Don't be tempted to let them try out the planes before the shoot-out, for the reasons given above. It can be fun to have a second test where all planes are used, but still try the selective approach first. To increase the energy boosting in good weather conditions, consider taking the participants outside to do this exercise. If there is a handy bridge, gallery or balcony the planes can be launched from, so much the better.

Team building	✪✪✪
Ice-breaking	✪
Energy	✪✪
Creativity	✪✪✪✪
Fun	✪✪✪

5.10 The wrong drawing

Preparation A number of pre-drawn objects on cards or flip-charts.
Running time Five to 10 minutes.
Environment Tables that partners sit either side of. If using a flip-chart, have desks arranged so that half the group has their back to it.
Teams Pairs.

Divide the group into pairs (see exercises 3.11 to 3.13) and have one of each pair nominated the describer and one the artist. The describer has to describe an object on the card or the flip-chart, but can only use geometric shapes, their orientation and position on the page in doing so. There must be no general comments about the overall subject or style. The artist then draws it, based on this description. The ideal situation is that the describer cannot see the drawing being produced.

For instance, a house might be drawn as a large square with a flattened triangle on top arranged in such a way that the long side of the triangle rests on and slightly overlaps the top edge of the square. It has four smaller squares inside the larger one... and so on. You can also see how difficult it would be to produce a drawing that has much more than the faintest resemblance to the original template.

Feedback The winners are the pair with a set of drawings most like the templates. Make sure that everyone has the opportunity to laugh at the efforts of all of their competitors.

Outcome This time-out is relatively low energy and is useful more as a way of switching away from the matter in hand than for building energy levels.

Variations It can be run with no preparation if you write up a subject to be drawn rather than draw a template picture. Templates can be taken from young children's colouring books to avoid unnecessary effort and artistic stress. If the numbers are relatively small, or space is limited, an alternative is to have a single describer with everyone else attempting to reproduce the same template.

Team building	✪✪
Ice-breaking	✪✪
Energy	✪✪
Creativity	✪✪✪
Fun	✪✪✪

5.11 Abstract drawing

Preparation None.
Running time Five to 10 minutes.
Environment Tables that partners sit either side of.
Teams Pairs.

Divide the group into pairs (see exercises 3.11 to 3.13) and have one of each pair nominated the describer and one the artist. The describer has to draw an object using at least one circle and at most 10 further lines. These lines need not be straight. The describer then relays verbally to the artist what he or she has drawn, using only geometric shapes and their orientation and position on the page. The artist attempts to reproduce the picture. The ideal situation is that the describer cannot see the drawing being produced. It is clear that the artist must not be able to see the original drawing.

Feedback This time-out works in exactly the same way as 'The wrong drawing' (5.10) but has a slight twist in that the describer can influence the complexity of the task. It has the advantage of requiring no preparation, but is more variable in result than 'The wrong drawing'.

Outcome The winners are the pair with a set of drawings most like each other. Make sure that everyone has the opportunity to laugh at the efforts of all of their competitors.

Variations It is clear that the circle and 10 lines are arbitrary. It is a simple matter to vary this. You could even make it specific to a particular subject by including a relevant shape in the list of requirements. An interesting variant is one where the set of objects used to construct the picture are specified beforehand (for example one circle, one triangle, two straight lines, two dots and one wiggly line). Both participants independently produce a picture using these objects, then compare results. If using this approach, let one person draw the picture first, attempt to 'project' the picture mentally to the other, then have the second draw their picture. It is probably best to combine one attempt using this independent approach with another using the describer/artist approach.

Team building	✪✪
Ice-breaking	✪✪
Energy	✪✪
Creativity	✪✪✪
Fun	✪✪✪

5.12 Magic square

Preparation None (or preparation of cards).
Running time Five minutes.
Environment A table for each participant or teams.
Teams Individual or small teams.

This can be run as a small team or as a solo activity depending upon your aims. If it is solo, you are setting up a useful mindset for independent mental work. If the exercise is undertaken in teams then the mindset is suitable for small team problem solving.

The objective is merely to construct a magic square using the numbers one to nine, arranged in a three-by-three grid in such a way that all horizontal, vertical and diagonal lines of three numbers add to 15.

The solution is:

8	3	4
1	5	9
6	7	2

and a rotation works as well:

2	7	6
9	5	1
4	3	8

Feedback You will probably discover that some find this activity trivial, while others find it hard. If this is the case, do not stop when the first one or two get a result, wait a while. The structure of the teams, if the exercise is run as a team activity, will be a factor in how fast a team achieves the answer.

Outcome This is a time-out that is useful for changing the mood and mindset of a group. If you have been involved in highly active group work and need to change pace and focus, use this. It can prove useful both in slightly damping down energy if a group is becoming too boisterous and in switching away from a subject which the group is finding difficult to let go.

Variations You can ask people to create the square by writing it on a sheet of paper or you could prepare sets of smaller cards that have the numbers one to nine on them. Having pre-prepared cards works best for groups, as everyone gets a chance to fight over where each card should go.

Team building	✪✪
Ice-breaking	✪
Energy	✪
Creativity	✪✪✪
Fun	✪✪

5.13 Let me tell you a story

Preparation None.
Running time 10 minutes.
Environment Room to sit in a circle, or at least in earshot of the whole group.
Teams Whole group.

In this time-out, the whole group comes together to tell a story. You select the theme of the story. Choose something that has many associations and strong imagery. It might be a traditional story theme in an unusual setting, or something entirely original. For example you could have 'Little Red Riding Hood goes to the annual shareholders' meeting' or 'Electric bananas'. You then ask someone to start and to pass the story on as soon as they have made it tough for the next person to follow. This could be after one sentence or a dozen.

The objective is that by the time you have gone right around the group, you have finished the story, you have made it as far-fetched as possible and you have stuck to the theme.

Feedback We have found with this time-out, as with many others, that using a mild sexually-related theme increases involvement.

Outcome You could use this time-out as the starting point for a creative idea generation session as a way of stimulating imagination. You could just use it as a way of being plain silly for a while.

Variations Most variations on this exercise involve different ways of switching storyteller. You can simply move around a circle. You can have the current storyteller choose the next one (to prevent participants a long way from the action switching off). The organizer can choose who is to speak next. You can have rules on exactly where the storyline breaks, to maximize humorous possibilities. For example, always ending on an adjective (except the last person). This allows for cliff-hangers like 'and she was holding an enormous…' and so forth. You could award points for laughter generated, for adherence to the theme or for stitching up the next in line.

Team building	✪✪
Ice-breaking	✪✪
Energy	✪✪
Creativity	✪✪✪✪
Fun	✪✪✪

5.14 Navigator

Preparation A map per team and a list of places.
Running time Five minutes.
Environment A table per team.
Teams One or more teams of two to six people.

Provide identical maps for each team. These could be road atlases, or even better, maps of around the scale 1:50,000. Before the activity, find five places on the map. They should be well separated. Some should be small villages or points of interest, others larger places. Either write the list of locations on a flip-chart or whiteboard, or provide a printed list for each team. The exercise is a race to see who can first get an itinerary to link the five places in the order you specify. Make it clear that it's up to them how they organize the activity between team members. If you only have a single team, the exercise becomes to complete the activity in five minutes.

Feedback As soon as a team has an itinerary, stop the activity. Get them to talk it through with the other teams following it on their maps and prepared to criticize. If there is a serious fault, the team is out of the running and the exercise continues. An appropriate prize (perhaps compasses for each member of the winning team) makes the activity more fun.

Outcome This isn't a high energy activity, but the team is engaged in a complex task – finding the five places and planning a route. As such, a significant part of the activity is working out how best to divide the task. Map-based activities are good for stimulating creative thought, so it makes a good time-out.

Variations With larger teams and two rooms, this can be a relay effort – split the team into two with a map each. The first team generates an itinerary without place names, which is relayed verbally to the second team, which has to recreate the list of places.

Team building	✪✪✪
Ice-breaking	✪
Energy	✪✪
Creativity	✪✪✪✪
Fun	✪✪

5.15 PR from hell

Preparation Think up one target per team.
Running time Five minutes.
Environment A table per team.
Teams Teams of two to six people.

Each team is given a target for which to produce a slogan. They have four minutes to devise an effective slogan, then each team tries out their slogan on the rest of the group. The winning slogan is rewarded. The catch here is that the target should be something that is particularly hard to sell. Try to make the targets as outrageous as possible, while bearing in mind your audience. Examples might be:

- Vlad the Impaler is running for mayor;
- selling cheap electronics to the Far East;
- an anti-flatulence tablet;
- selling paper warships to the navy.

Feedback If there's time, get the teams to describe how they reached their slogan. Often initial hilarity will lead to a dry patch. How did they get their result? Was it democratic or autocratic? Was it a team effort or individual within the team? There is no right answer here, we're just helping them understand how they work together.

Outcome The sillier you can make the targets, the more energy you are liable to induce. This is a good time-out to revitalize creative thought, as the feedback pushes the participants into thinking about how they work together.

Variations The exercise works slightly better with different targets for each team, but can be used on a single subject. To keep it short we've limited the output to producing a snappy slogan, but there are a number of variations here. With more time, your teams could produce an advertising jingle, a full-scale advertisement, a press release or a newspaper advert. It is worth emphasizing if acting is involved that they are best sticking to 'straight' acting. Intentional comedy is extremely hard for amateurs to make work, and whatever they do will be unintentionally funny anyway.

Team building	✪✪✪
Ice-breaking	✪✪
Energy	✪✪✪
Creativity	✪✪✪✪
Fun	✪✪✪

5.16 Passing the buck

Preparation One tennis ball sized ball.
Running time Three minutes.
Environment No special requirements.
Teams Whole group.

Give the ball to one member of the group. Their task is to get the ball around the whole team in such a way that it does not pass on to the person sitting next to them. Do not make any suggestion that they move away from seats, tables, etc. Time the activity. Tell them how long it took, and ask them to halve it. When they've had another go, ask them to get it down to three seconds.

Feedback If someone doesn't spot it, give them a hint after a while that they needn't stay seated or in the same positions. Most of the ways of speeding up the exercise involve changing from throwing the ball (and dropping it) to quick means of passing it – for instance a slightly sloping row of hands down which the ball is rolled. The quickest means is for them all to get round the ball and touch it at roughly (though inevitably not exactly) the same time.

Outcome The principle aim here (and it's one that is worth explicitly pointing out) is to spot that the restrictions which stop us from achieving something are often self-imposed. No-one said that they had to stay in position, but almost always the first attempt or two will involve doing so. It is also interesting (and again worth pointing out) that moving the goal posts a bit (halving the time) often doesn't generate a creative solution, while moving them a long way does. For good measure, it also shows that what is initially assumed is impossible often is not. Despite all this learning, it does inject a small amount of energy too.

Variations There aren't many obvious variations, though obviously the object passed could be almost anything, though it should be small and non-delicate enough to encourage an original inclination to throw it (a frisbee, for instance).

Team building	✪✪✪
Ice-breaking	✪
Energy	✪✪
Creativity	✪✪✪✪
Fun	✪✪✪

5.17 What a load of dross

Preparation None.
Running time 10 minutes (or as long as it will run).
Environment A room with a flip-chart that all the participants can see.
Teams Group of any size.

The only objective is to generate as many reasons as possible that a product, range of products, or a service is dross (use a more explicit term here if the group is not likely to be offended). If the target can be the best product or service that the company offers, so much the better.

Feedback There is very little that is as energizing as dishing the dirt on someone or something. This warm-up really involves people and gets them ready for a session that will put right some of the drawbacks they have identified.

Outcome This type of time-out provides a particularly valuable lead-in to an idea generation session, particularly one focusing on product improvement. There are two obvious outcomes. The first is that the energy is raised and the group gets into a frame of mind that makes shouting out ideas okay. The second is that you generate a list of development areas that can be used as raw material for a problem solving session.

Variations The time-out can be run as an end in itself or could be used as a source of raw material for the main session. The subject matter can be varied in all sorts of ways. The only really important factor is that it should focus on the negative. The exercise can equally be applied to your competitors' products or to your own. If the only aim is to bring a team together, use a competitors' product, or even better your company policies, rules and restrictions as a target. If you are working on product improvement, make sure you are pulling apart your own products and services, however painful this may be.

Team building	✪✪✪✪
Ice-breaking	✪✪
Energy	✪✪
Creativity	✪✪✪✪
Fun	✪✪✪

5.18 Strange tools

Preparation A sheet of paper per team.
Running time 10 minutes.
Environment No specific requirements.
Teams One or more teams of between three and six people.

Pick a specific, concrete problem. Make it dramatic – building Stonehenge, setting the leaning tower of Pisa straight, etc. This is the problem for all the teams.

Each team passes round a sheet of paper from person to person. The first person writes 'A' and folds the sheet over so whatever was written is hidden. The second person writes an adjective (eg big, green, etc) and folds over again. The third writes a noun (eg spanner, sausage). The next writes 'with', the next another adjective, and so on. Make sure you have a large enough chain of words so that everyone writes something (the paper passes round again if the team is too small). The easiest way to plan this out is to write a description of a bizarre tool first, and use this as the model of the type of word required at each stage. For example, 'A large electric mincer with heavy blades which runs on wheels'.

The team now unfolds its sheet and spends a one-minute session deciding just how this unlikely tool could be used to solve the problem. The solutions are then shared with the whole group, and the most entertaining wins a prize.

Feedback Emphasize how it has been possible to solve the problem (admittedly with drastic flaws) using the most inappropriate tools, and certainly not one they would originally have thought of. Stress the need for coming at a problem from a totally unexpected direction if the usual means are failing.

Outcome The process of solving a problem with a strange tool is not the real benefit here. The exercise is not intended to produce a real solution (hence the value of a prize), but to get the participants into a problem-solving frame of mind.

Variations The strange tool could be generated in various ways, for instance by using a computer program or different words on rotating concentric cardboard circles.

Team building	✪✪✪
Ice-breaking	✪
Energy	✪✪
Creativity	✪✪✪✪
Fun	✪✪✪

6

HI-TECH AND HI-PREP

HERE'S ONE I MADE EARLIER

Most of the exercises in Chapter 5 require relatively little preparation. However, some of the most effective exercises do need a little work beforehand – it is more than repaid by the impact a dramatic exercise can have. Sometimes, it's just a matter of making a standard exercise more effective. For example, the time-out 'A to Z' (5.8) can be significantly improved by preparing flip-charts or whiteboards with lists of letters from A to Z. These can be prepared before the event, or during a coffee or lunch break.

This chapter, though, looks beyond the basic enhancement to exercises which simply won't function without a significant amount of preparation. This may be on your part, involved in producing or laying out the material for the exercise, or could be a delegated activity like having a PC and video projector or other technology available on the day.

THE PREPARATION TOOL BAG

Before going into the specific exercises, consider whether it would be helpful to put together an instant teamwork tool bag. This would provide you with handy resources to undertake some of the simpler exercises requiring preparation without actually using up any time on the day. If you are frequently involved in running meetings, in training or in development, this would be extremely valuable.

The specific tool bag you require will vary significantly depending on the sort of activities you undertake, but the typical contents might be:

- whiteboard pens (several sets);
- different coloured pieces of string;
- scissors;
- adhesive tape;
- flipchart paper;
- water pistols;
- blindfolds (sleep masks are good for this);
- a timer – such as a stopwatch or kitchen timer;
- a noisemaker (eg air horn or smoke alarm).

Water pistols or soft foam balls can make excellent props to accompany many exercises. Anything that requires someone to stop after a specific time (or when they get boring) can be given an extra frisson by arming the audience with instructions to fire if the speaker strays from the specification.

A final general purpose tool is the instant camera. This could be a traditional type, like a Polaroid, one of the widely available digital cameras with a PC to support it, or a video camera plus TV if neither of these are available. The instant camera has a specific role to play in some of the exercises in this chapter, but it is also valuable to capture interesting moments in almost any of the exercises. Such shots, if used correctly, can be helpful to boost team spirit and togetherness. It's important that the pictures aren't seen as a threat, for showing the rest of the world, but rather as something that belongs to 'us'.

6.1 People chain

Preparation Before the event, each person provides a single paragraph on their experience and interests. These are spread around the room (or larger area if possible) on individual sheets (A sheets). Derive a unique piece of information about each person and produce a second sheet (B sheets) with this information on it, but someone else's name at the top. Place these around the area too.
Running time A minute per team member
Environment Any room format with plenty of wall space, the larger the better.
Teams Individual, ideally between eight and 30 people.

Make sure that each member of the group has paper and pen. Their task is to produce a chain of names. First they should find the B sheet with their own name on it. This will have someone else's key information below. They must find out whose information this is, writing the second name down on the paper after their own. They then find the B sheet with this second person's name on to get the next clue. Using this technique, they follow round the chain. The A sheets provide background information. By browsing them, the participants can discover the information they need.

Feedback It is excessive (and embarrassing) to keep the session running until the last person has completed the chain. Wait for the first three and stop the exercise. Get them to read through their name chains (you should have one prepared beforehand) to check them.

Outcome In the rush to find links, it is easy to miss how much you are getting to know about the individuals involved. This exercise provides some early ice-breaking, and is particularly effective with a session involving a stay away from base.

Variations Although not essential, it helps to have pictures of the participants on the A sheets. If you can't get them beforehand, consider using a digital camera to get quick shots into the sheets. If you have a little more time, have each person find their own A sheet at the end and read it out to the rest, reinforcing the link.

Team building	✪✪
Ice-breaking	✪✪✪✪
Energy	✪✪✪
Creativity	✪✪
Fun	✪✪✪

6.2 Contract fishing

Preparation A large number of sheets of paper with paper-clips taped to them (at least 10 sheets per team). If the papers can be in the form of spoof contracts, so much the better. For each team a stick with a longish piece of string attached (2–3 metres) and a magnet fixed to the end of the string.
Running time Five minutes.
Environment Any room format where a small section of the room can have a row of tables placed across it.
Teams At least two and preferably no more than five or six per team.

Make a barrier with tables, and place all the sheets of paper on the floor on the far side of the barrier. Give each team a fishing pole. Describe the scenario: the company has decided to allow all groups in the company to tender for any work required. Rather than go through the time-consuming business of requests to tender, all contracts are placed in a pool. Whichever team fishes out a contract gets to undertake it. An individual in the team will be fishing: at regular intervals you will ask them to hand over the rod, until everyone has had a go. During the process notify them at the intervals necessitated by the team size when to hand over the pole. Get the rest of the team to encourage the fisher.

Feedback Count up the contracts each team has and award the winner some sort of prize. Point out that, while this is probably a good way to allocate contracts, to make it effective, they would have to have the option of throwing a contract back if they didn't want it.

Outcome This can generate a lot of energy, especially when more than one person goes for the same contract.

Variations For a longer, more thought-provoking version, each contract should be labelled with a duration and a value. The team can only hold contracts with (say) 100 duration points. Their aim is to maximize value, and they can throw contracts back into the pool.

Team building	✪✪
Ice-breaking	✪✪
Energy	✪✪✪✪
Creativity	✪✪
Fun	✪✪✪✪

6.3 Surfing the net

Preparation One PC per team, connected to the Internet. Five unlikely pieces of information. Web addresses of three search engines.
Running time 15 minutes.
Environment Tables so each team can get comfortably round a PC screen.
Teams At least two with preferably no more than four people per team.

Write the search engine addresses on a whiteboard or flip-chart. Also put up five requests for information. They should be concise and obscure. For example:

- the name of the fourth episode of the third season of the *X-Files*;
- the name of a piece of music by Ligetti;
- the atomic weight of Polonium;
- winner of the 1964 Academy Award for best picture.

At the end of the sessions, teams are expected to have answers to all the questions, plus to have found the wackiest web site. When the five questions are answered they should register this, but continue searching for an unusual site. Allow ten minutes for searching, then get feedback. You could rotate keyboard operators every two minutes.

Feedback Each team shouts out their wacky address and the other teams browse to it. Take a vote of the teams on which is the best site – if they can't agree, overrule them. Prizes for the first team to complete and the oddest site.

Outcome This isn't a high energy activity, but it is very effective as a time-out when your group has been focusing very hard on a specific topic and needs to think of something completely different. It also demonstrates the effectiveness of the Internet to those less familiar with it, so provides some instant learning too.

Variations You can bring the time down to 10 minutes by only doing the wacky site search – in fact five minutes pure browsing can be a very effective time-out, provided everyone has their own PC. However, to keep the interest of a team there needs to be more of a competitive element.

Team building	✪✪
Ice-breaking	✪
Energy	✪✪
Creativity	✪✪✪
Fun	✪✪✪

6.4 Snapshots

Preparation Instant camera, digital camera or video camera. Half an hour site visit. Rough maps.
Running time 10 minutes.
Environment No special requirements.
Teams At least two. Preferably no more than six per team.

Before the exercise, take five shots around the location of the session using one of the technologies suggested in the preparation section. The pictures should be of something which is clearly identified, but not easily spotted. The places that are pictured should be outside the meeting room, but within a very short walking distance. The teams are given a rough map of the area and are shown the five images. Their task is to mark on the map where the five images are located.

Feedback If a team gets all five images before time allowed is up, you could have a bonus image up your sleeve to keep them occupied. The team which gets all five first, or comes closest wins a prize.

Outcome Snapshots is a great multipurpose activity, getting people moving, out of the meeting room and searching in a creative manner.

Variations A number of variants are possible here. You can show all five images up front, or have one image on show for the first two minutes, one for the next two minutes and so on (this means the teams have to manage time better). If the images are shown up front, you could repeat them throughout, or you could have two or three viewing sessions through the event. An inversion of this exercise requiring considerably more equipment and quite a bit more time is possible. Note down on a sheet a number of interesting items or views around the meeting room. Each team is sent out with some form of instant camera, and has to return with shots of as many of the required targets as possible. This variant is particularly challenging because you can include mobile targets like people.

Team building	✪✪✪
Ice-breaking	✪
Energy	✪✪✪✪
Creativity	✪✪✪
Fun	✪✪✪✪

6.5 *Fontastic*

Preparation Digital camera plus PC, or video camera and TV per team.
Running time 10 minutes.
Environment Enough room for each team to have at least 2 metres square of clear floor area – ideally in separate rooms.
Teams At least two with four to five people per team.

Each team has to produce a body font and capture it on digital camera or video. To do this, the team members spell out as many capital letters of the alphabet as they can, using only their bodies. One member of the team captures each letter using the camera (if using video, just a couple of seconds on each letter, not a video of the whole process). The role of camera operator must rotate every time to make sure everyone takes part.

Feedback The winning team is the one with the most legible letters – if there's a draw, decide on the quality of the font.

Outcome This can be a riotously noisy activity, so make sure the environment is conducive to it. There's lots of energy and ice-breaking (difficult not to when you've been in such contortions together).

Variations It is possible to use this activity without the cameras as a true instant exercise, in which case it could appear in any of the three categories. However, it works much better with the cameras, as otherwise the participants don't get to see their own letters, nor the activities of the other teams, and this is a major part of the value. Other variants are to get the teams to produce numbers or pictures using their bodies. This last option is valuable if you haven't enough resources to have small teams – making letters with a big team is less challenging, but making a picture of a house is more stretching. The exercise is more intimate if the participants have to lie on the floor, rather than attempt the letters standing up – you may wish to make this a requirement.

Team building	✪✪✪✪
Ice-breaking	✪✪✪
Energy	✪✪✪✪
Creativity	✪✪✪✪
Fun	✪✪✪✪

6.6 Bomb alert

Preparation One briefcase or box with combination lock and up to four very long pieces of string per team. For each number on the combination, a clue should be fixed to the wall.
Running time 10 minutes.
Environment A large room, ideally with other usable rooms connecting directly to it.
Teams No more than five per team.

The teams are bomb disposal experts. Their task is to disarm a bomb by entering the correct code into the device. There is only one chance to get it right. One member of the team is left with the bomb; the others find the code. Once they leave the secure area, they can't return or speak as this may trigger the bomb's sensitive mechanism. Luckily each team member has a piece of string. They hold one end; the person with the bomb holds the other. The team is allowed to talk to establish how they will use the string to communicate. They then leave the bombsite and can no longer speak.

Clues should be cryptic, but simple. For example Bomb A, digit 1 – square root of 64 (or add together the two numbers of the sides of a dodecahedron, or Jerome K. Jerome's X men in a boat). When the full combination is entered, the bomb holder holds up his hand, the whole team comes back to the centre and the case is opened or… catastrophe.

Feedback As an incentive you can put a small prize, like a bag of sweets, in the case. Don't stop just because one team has finished, but have a strict time limit with regular announcements of progress – the bomb will blow up after 10 minutes if it has not been disabled.

Outcome This is a good combination of team strengthening, energy building from movement and tension, and creativity stimulation.

Variations If possible, have a loud sound effect (eg an air horn or smoke alarm) ready when you monitor the combination being input. If the combination is wrong, blast them with noise. If the scene has been set effectively this should make them jump.

Team building	✪✪✪
Ice-breaking	✪✪
Energy	✪✪✪
Creativity	✪✪✪✪
Fun	✪✪✪✪

6.7 Rules rule

Preparation An over-sized pack of cards or a PC with projector and a program to throw up random cards.
Running time Five minutes.
Environment Any arrangement, provided all participants can see the cards.
Teams Individual.

Turn a card up and put it to one side. Then 'play' the remaining cards. Each one is turned up alongside the original card. You then state whether the card is valid or not, and discard it. The card is valid if it fits the rules of the game, but the group does not know the rules. Their task is to deduce the rules. As soon as someone feels they know what is happening, stop the process and listen to their theory. If it is true, the exercise is finished. If not, continue until someone can describe the rules.

Rules are up to you, but must be applied consistently. Examples might be 'the card must follow a card of a different suit', or 'a card must be bigger in value than the previous card'. If this proves too easy, join rules, for example 'a red must follow a black unless it is a face card, in which case it can follow anything'.

Feedback Have a number of rules in reserve. If the rule is deduced quickly, say that was a practice round and run again with a more complex rule. If someone guesses wrong, point out the dangers of making assumptions with incomplete evidence – but a timely guess may win the game.

Outcome This is an effective way of warming up the creative juices, but warn the participants that an analytical approach is not ideal in the early stages of creativity, when it is best to ignore rules, logic and practicality.

Variations The same principle can be applied to anything where a rule can be deduced. Numerous physical puzzles can be used, for example a box with holes in, where a marble is dropped in one hole and emerges from another and the participants have to deduce the internal structure of the box. Such hands-on variants are best done with a number of artefacts, working in small teams.

Team building	✪
Ice-breaking	✪
Energy	✪✪
Creativity	✪✪✪✪
Fun	✪✪✪

6.8 Racing demon

Preparation A pack of playing cards per person.
Running time 10 minutes.
Environment One or more tables.
Teams One or more with at least four, and not more than 10, per team.

This once-popular game works well as a warm-up. Each team member has a pack of cards. Each shuffles their pack and places 13 cards face down on the table. When they are ready, a nominated person says 'go'. The players turn up the top card of the 13. The aim is to be the first to dispose of these 13 cards (the demon). They are removed by building piles of cards of the same suit from Ace to King in the centre of the playing area. All piles are shared – anyone can put a card on any pile (but an Ace must be used to start it). To make this action more practical, the player can also play from the remainder of the pack in traditional patience (solitaire) fashion – by turning over three cards at a time, and if the card uncovered will fit on a pile it can be played. Make sure that participants understand that there are no turns – you play as fast as you can.

Feedback A quick demonstration may be useful. As soon as one player in the team has disposed of the 13 cards, play stops.

Outcome It might seem that a card game is unlikely to raise energy, but the need to watch many different spots for the opportunity to play makes this a very intense game. Make the players stand for extra energy.

Variations In the full game, play stops when the first demon is disposed of, but the winner is decided by counting up the number of cards each person has played. Everyone but the player without a demon subtracts twice the number of cards left in their demon from their total. This makes the game more tactical, but involves a longer finish, reducing the impact as warm-up. It also requires that each pack has a different back pattern so cards can be counted.

Team building	✪
Ice-breaking	✪✪
Energy	✪✪✪
Creativity	✪✪✪
Fun	✪✪✪✪

6.9 *The web chain*

Preparation A PC with Internet connection per team. Recent check of Web sites.
Running time 10 minutes.
Environment A table for each team.
Teams Two or more with one to four people per team.

The aim of the exercise is to get from one World Wide Web site (with the address given) to another (unknown). The route is indicated by a set of clues, each pointing to one of a number of intermediate sites. Most Web sites have links to other sites. Your preparation will involve you in finding a starting site, then wandering along a chain of connections. Make sure some sites have a good number of links. Then think of a suitable cryptic clue to make it clear which link the team is to use. For example, if a link points to a hot air balloon manufacturer, you might say 'this firm's products could be inflated by politicians'. The first team to get the goal site on screen is the winner.

Feedback You don't want the same person to be 'driving' the PC throughout the exercise, or the other members will get limited value. Divide the time by the number of people on the biggest team and at appropriate intervals get them to move on to the next person. This will be particularly helpful if the teams consist of a mix of Internet novices and experts.

Outcome Simply exposing the players to the different Web sites (try to make them as bizarre and fun as possible – use a 'cool sites' listing to find some) will provide launching points for creative thought. If you don't know how to do this, check the 'creativity now' entry on the Creativity Unleashed Limited creativity page, http://www.cul.co.uk/creative. Team interaction in working the clues will help get people working together better.

Variations Note the need to check as close to the event as possible that the chain is still viable; Web sites change without warning. In the event of a broken chain, be prepared to jump over one link.

Team building	✪✪✪
Ice-breaking	✪✪
Energy	✪✪
Creativity	✪✪✪✪
Fun	✪✪✪

6.10 Treasure hunt

Preparation Four items of the same type per team, different colours for each team, placed around the playing area. (Optionally) map of the playing area.
Running time 10 minutes.
Environment Large area where teams can move freely.
Teams As many as required with two to four people.

Split the group into teams. The objective is to be first back with their four items. Each team has the same types of item, but in different colours. Brightly coloured pieces of string (easy to tie in place) or balloons are effective. You will need to set up the playing area beforehand, distributing the objects to be found. This requires some subtlety. If the activity area is in use (we have performed this exercise in hotels and offices), the objects need to be possible to find, but not so obvious that passers-by remove them. The teams should return in five minutes, even if they haven't got all four objects. You may find it useful to have a map of the playing area, to limit the time taken and to avoid teams straying into areas they shouldn't.

Feedback Small prizes for everyone, but slightly better ones for the first teams back, work well. It is particularly effective if you can have some sort of activity (puzzles, for instance) for the first teams back to undertake, in case they have to wait a few minutes for the rest.

Outcome There's lots of movement in this one, and it gets everyone out of the room. This can be doubly useful as it pushes up the energy (particularly if the room has bad air conditioning) and also because it gives you time to prepare for other parts of the event or meeting.

Variations In the basic version, teams are sent out without specific instructions about staying together. A good variant is asking them to stay in a group, and reinforcing this by saying they should hold hands at all times. This adds an interesting challenge to the exercise and provides some team building, especially if the exercise is in a public place.

Team building	✪✪✪
Ice-breaking	✪
Energy	✪✪✪✪
Creativity	✪✪
Fun	✪✪✪✪

6.11 Lego™ construction

Preparation Lego™ bricks, a simple Lego™ construction to copy and blindfolds.
Running time 10 to 15 minutes.
Environment At least two rooms.
Teams Four people per team.

The object of the warm-up is to copy a simple Lego™ structure. Divide the group into teams: one is the eyes, one is the mouth, two are the hands, arms and legs.

The eyes can see what is being copied but can't speak and can't see what is being built. The mouth can speak and can see what is being built, but can't see what is being copied. The hands arms and legs can't see (they wear blindfolds).

In one room the eyes look at the original structure, then pass instructions to the mouth. The mouth directs the hands, arms and legs through the building process using these instructions. The mouth can't touch the Lego™ bricks or fellow team members.

The first team to complete the construction accurately wins. Unless you have extra time, ignore the colour of the bricks.

Feedback In this warm-up, you are dependent upon your fellow team members. It is frustrating when there is a bottleneck. It often seems that you could do the job better on your own. Some roles cause members of the team to feel excluded and it is easy to leave them this way. When you are under pressure it is easy to focus on the task and tough to think of the team members.

Outcome With a discussion session afterwards, this warm-up provides important teamworking lessons.

Variations The division of the team is arbitrary, as is its size. You could run it with teams of three (one constructor) or introduce additional roles into the process. If you wanted to build in lessons about communication, you should forbid note taking and could introduce additional steps between the eyes and the mouth.

Team building	✪✪✪✪
Ice-breaking	✪✪
Energy	✪✪✪
Creativity	✪✪✪
Fun	✪✪✪✪

6.12 Nonsense object

Preparation A selection of bizarre objects, eg traffic cones, large foam shapes.
Running time 10 minutes.
Environment Space for all participants to see one another and some room for movement.
Teams Individual; group can be any size.

You need a selection of large, bizarre objects that can provide a spark for the imagination. The challenge for the participants is to step forward, take one of the objects and act out a scene with it. In other words, the object, which is in itself meaningless, is used as a prop to become something else.

The activity finishes when everyone has had a go. If the group is large, it is worth limiting the exercise to around six or seven participants, selected at random.

Feedback To really get this game firing on all cylinders you need one or two people in the group who are prepared to step forward and make fools of themselves. Others tend to join in as they get the idea. If you have a group that is largely made up of uninhibited extroverts it will really take off and you may need extra time if the group is large.

Outcome This is a very funny warm-up and tends to be involving. Since it relies on wit there will be individuals within a group who will find it tough. It is generally best not to pressure them.

Variations You may find it effective to have a time limit (perhaps 45 seconds) for each individual, with water pistols or other weapons available should they over-run. As described, the participants can choose any prop. It is possible to pre-assign them so that each individual must work with the prop you give them. It also works well to pre-assign the props but to allow people to swap when they see a use for another person's. The activity can also be undertaken on a team basis, with one team member acting out a scene to the others. If this approach is used, the objects should rotate around the teams, with different team members taking turns to use different objects.

Team building	✪✪
Ice-breaking	✪✪
Energy	✪✪✪✪
Creativity	✪✪✪✪
Fun	✪✪✪

7

OTHER SOURCES

It will become obvious, as you dip into this book, that we have collected our warm-ups, time-outs and ice-breakers from a wide variety of sources. Many we have gleaned from other facilitators and trainers, some we have adapted from children's games and some we have made up ourselves. We haven't taken any directly from other books but it is inevitable that there will be some overlap, particularly in those that we have learnt from other people.

We are keen that you should expand your repertoire beyond the activities in this book. The easiest source for you will be other trainers or facilitators. They have an advantage over books in that you can ask for their favourites – that way you get tried and tested ideas rather than just something from a list. (The exercises in *Instant Teamwork* are almost all tried and tested favourites.) Next ask young children for their favourite party games. They will often choose high action, high energy games that can be easily adapted.

The next best source will be other books. We have listed some book sources below. While looking in books you would also benefit from expanding your search and reading books of children's games and party games.

Once you have developed a wide range of activities you need to think about where to source materials. Obviously toy stores are a must. Large stores like Toys R Us will give inspiration as you walk around them. If you live in the United States, Archie McPhee (www.mcphee.com) is a great source for really off-the-wall toys and other materials (items are available via the web site, but outside the United States and Canada the postage will probably be prohibitive). When it comes to more basic materials such as string, rope and duct tape, do-it-yourself stores will be useful places to visit. Finally, the more basic facilitation material such as pens, paper, card, glue, scissors, etc can be found at stationery stores.

BOOKS

Leslie Bendaly, *Games Teams Play*, McGraw-Hill, 1996.

Rex Davies and David McDermott, *Mind-Opening Training Games*, McGraw-Hill, 1996.

Gary Kroehnert, *100 Training Games*, McGraw-Hill, 1992.

Ken Jones, *Icebreakers: A Sourcebook of Games, Exercises, and Stimulations*, Gulf, 1997.

Rod Napier, *Advanced Games for Trainers*, McGraw-Hill, 1998.

John Newstrom and Edward Scannell, *Games Trainers Play*, McGraw-Hill, 1989.

John Newstrom and Edward Scannell, *Even More Games Trainers Play*, McGraw-Hill, 1994.

John Newstrom and Edward Scannell, *The Big Book of Business Games*, McGraw-Hill, 1996.

Carolyn Nilson, *Team Games for Trainers*, McGraw-Hill, 1993.

Carolyn Nilson, *More Team Games for Trainers*, McGraw-Hill, 1997.

WEB SOURCES

It is always risky putting World Wide Web resources into a book because the web moves far faster than printed material ever can. The very best way to find tips and techniques is to use a search engine such as Yahoo (www.yahoo.com) or Altavista (www.altavista.digital.com). We have included a couple of references here that will give you an indication of the sorts of things that are available.

First, take a look at the Creativity Unleashed Limited site (www.cul.co.uk) for ideas and inspiration. Also, look at the Idea Exchange in the Idea Zone (www.ideazone.com). As the title suggests, there are a number of good ideas to be found here. Smart Biz (www.smartbiz.com) has a wide range of useful business information. There is at least one section that will be of relevance and the search engine on the site can help you find it and others.

A very specific address that will no doubt have changed sometime after this book is published is wiuadm1.wiu.edu/miosa/Lessons/warm-ups.htm.

Finally, while using the search engines, don't forget to look in Usenet – the Internet's version of online bulletin boards. The misc.business.facilitators group often has some interesting and useful discussions.

APPENDIX: THE SELECTOR

This appendix contains a set of tables that will help you to find the activity that best suits your needs. The first entry is a random selector. This can be effective if you aren't sure where to start, or you feel you are getting stuck in a rut. The next set of tables are sorted by the star ratings for each activity, to make it easy to pick out (say) a high energy activity. Finally come tables sorted by preparation time and running time.

THE RANDOM SELECTOR

Take a watch with a second hand and note the number the second hand is pointing at now. Take that number activity from the list of 60 below. These are almost all from Chapters 3 to 5, but exclude a few ice-breaking activities which are simply designed to pair up, and include three of the higher preparation activities from Chapter 6 which can work with relatively little preparation.

No.	Ref.	Title
1	3.1	This is my friend
2	3.2	Tower of Babel
3	3.3	Yes!
4	3.4	Something for the weekend
5	3.5	Follow my leader
6	3.6	Spoon and string
7	3.7	Piggyback plus
8	3.8	Row of eyes
9	3.9	True and false
10	3.10	I am and I know
11	3.14	Trust me, I'll catch you
12	3.15	Sit on my lap
13	3.16	Sense and sensibility
14	3.17	You're an animal
15	3.18	You're great because...
16	4.1	The paper-clip race
17	4.2	Balloon volleyball
18	4.3	The magic tunnel
19	4.4	Bursting with energy
20	4.5	On the square
21	4.6	Knots
22	4.7	Handcuffs
23	4.8	Makeover
24	4.9	Boy meets girl
25	4.10	Steeplechase
26	4.11	Circle of energy
27	4.12	Beam me up
28	4.13	One spare square
29	4.14	The people machine
30	4.15	Elastic band race
31	4.16	Sheepdog trials
32	4.17	Magic carpet
33	4.18	Balloon racing
34	4.19	Out for the count
35	4.20	Cow tails

36	4.21	Peer groups
37	4.22	Giants, witches and dwarves
38	4.23	Suck and blow
39	4.24	Magnet race
40	5.1	Towering
41	5.2	Ands
42	5.3	Tongue twisters
43	5.4	Buy me
44	5.5	Blindfold birthday
45	5.6	Animals
46	5.7	Ideas to get you fired
47	5.8	A to Z
48	5.9	Plane sailing
49	5.10	The wrong drawing
50	5.11	Abstract drawing
51	5.12	Magic square
52	5.13	Let me tell you a story
53	5.14	Navigator
54	5.15	PR from hell
55	5.16	Passing the buck
56	5.17	What a load of dross
57	5.18	Strange tools
58	6.5	Fontastic
59	6.7	Rules rule
60	6.10	Treasure hunt

ACTIVITIES IN TEAMWORK ORDER

This table sorts the activities by the teamwork star ratings attached to each. Those at the top have the highest star rating, those at the bottom the lowest.

Ref.	Title
	✪✪✪✪
3.16	Sense and sensibility
3.18	You're great because...
5.1	Towering
5.17	What a load of dross
6.5	Fontastic
6.11	Lego construction
	✪✪✪
3.2	Tower of Babel
3.3	Yes!
3.5	Follow my leader
3.7	Piggyback plus
3.8	Row of eyes
3.9	True and false
3.14	Trust me, I'll catch you
3.15	Sit on my lap
3.17	You're an animal
4.1	The paper-clip race
4.2	Balloon volleyball
4.3	The magic tunnel
4.5	On the square
4.6	Knots
4.8	Makeover
4.9	Boy meets girl
4.11	Circle of energy
4.13	One spare square
4.14	The people machine
4.15	Elastic band race
4.16	Sheepdog trials
4.17	Magic carpet
4.22	Giants, witches and dwarves
5.3	Tongue twisters
5.5	Blindfold birthday
5.7	Ideas to get you fired
5.9	Plane sailing
5.14	Navigator

5.15 PR from hell
5.16 Passing the buck
5.18 Strange tools
6.4 Snapshots
6.6 Bomb alert
6.9 The web chain
6.10 Treasure hunt

✪✪

3.1 This is my friend
3.4 Something for the weekend
3.6 Spoon and string
3.10 I am and I know
3.11 Pairing hands
3.12 Keys in the ring
3.13 String in the box
4.4 Bursting with energy
4.7 Handcuffs
4.10 Steeplechase
4.12 Beam me up
4.18 Balloon racing
4.20 Cow tails
4.23 Suck and blow
4.24 Magnet race
5.6 Animals
5.8 A to Z
5.10 The wrong drawing
5.11 Abstract drawing
5.12 Magic square
5.13 Let me tell you a story
6.1 People chain
6.2 Contract fishing
6.3 Surfing the net
6.12 Nonsense object

✪

4.19 Out for the count
4.21 Peer groups
5.2 Ands
5.4 Buy me
6.7 Rules rule
6.8 Racing demon

ACTIVITIES IN ICE-BREAKING ORDER

This table sorts the activities by the ice-breaking star ratings attached to each. Those at the top have the highest star rating, those at the bottom the lowest.

Ref.	Title
	✪✪✪✪
3.1	This is my friend
3.4	Something for the weekend
3.5	Follow my leader
3.6	Spoon and string
3.8	Row of eyes
3.9	True and false
3.16	Sense and sensibility
3.17	You're an animal
3.18	You're great because...
6.1	People chain
	✪✪✪
3.2	Tower of Babel
3.3	Yes!
3.7	Piggyback plus
3.10	I am and I know
3.14	Trust me, I'll catch you
4.7	Handcuffs
4.8	Makeover
4.23	Suck and blow
5.5	Blindfold birthday
6.5	Fontastic
	✪✪
3.11	Pairing hands
3.12	Keys in the ring
3.13	String in the box
3.15	Sit on my lap
4.1	The paper-clip race
4.4	Bursting with energy
4.5	On the square
4.6	Knots
4.11	Circle of energy
4.12	Beam me up
4.13	One spare square
4.15	Elastic band race

4.16	Sheepdog trials
4.17	Magic carpet
4.19	Out for the count
4.20	Cow tails
4.21	Peer groups
4.22	Giants, witches and dwarves
5.1	Towering
5.2	Ands
5.3	Tongue twisters
5.4	Buy me
5.6	Animals
5.10	The wrong drawing
5.11	Abstract drawing
5.13	Let me tell you a story
5.15	PR from hell
5.17	What a load of dross
6.2	Contract fishing
6.6	Bomb alert
6.8	Racing demon
6.9	The web chain
6.11	Lego™ construction
6.12	Nonsense object

✪

4.2	Balloon volleyball
4.3	The magic tunnel
4.9	Boy meets girl
4.10	Steeplechase
4.14	The people machine
4.18	Balloon racing
4.24	Magnet race
5.7	Ideas to get you fired
5.8	A to Z
5.9	Plane sailing
5.12	Magic square
5.14	Navigator
5.16	Passing the buck
5.18	Strange tools
6.3	Surfing the net
6.4	Snapshots
6.7	Rules rule
6.10	Treasure hunt

ACTIVITIES IN ENERGY ORDER

This table sorts the activities by the energy star ratings attached to each. Those at the top have the highest star rating, those at the bottom the lowest.

Ref.	Title
	✪✪✪✪
3.7	Piggyback plus
3.10	I am and I know
3.15	Sit on my lap
4.1	The paper-clip race
4.2	Balloon volleyball
4.4	Bursting with energy
4.5	On the square
4.6	Knots
4.10	Steeplechase
4.11	Circle of energy
4.12	Beam me up
4.13	One spare square
4.14	The people machine
4.15	Elastic band race
4.16	Sheepdog trials
4.17	Magic carpet
4.21	Peer groups
4.22	Giants, witches and dwarves
5.5	Blindfold birthday
6.2	Contract fishing
6.4	Snapshots
6.5	Fontastic
6.10	Treasure hunt
6.12	Nonsense object
	✪✪✪
3.2	Tower of Babel
3.3	Yes!
3.5	Follow my leader
3.6	Spoon and string
3.9	True and false
3.11	Pairing hands
3.12	Keys in the ring
3.13	String in the box
3.14	Trust me, I'll catch you
3.16	Sense and sensibility

3.17	You're an animal
4.3	The magic tunnel
4.7	Handcuffs
4.8	Makeover
4.9	Boy meets girl
4.18	Balloon racing
4.19	Out for the count
4.20	Cow tails
4.23	Suck and blow
4.24	Magnet race
5.1	Towering
5.3	Tongue twisters
5.4	Buy me
5.6	Animals
5.8	A to Z
5.15	PR from hell
6.1	People chain
6.6	Bomb alert
6.8	Racing demon
6.11	Lego™ construction
	✪✪
3.1	This is my friend
3.4	Something for the weekend
3.8	Row of eyes
5.2	Ands
5.7	Ideas to get you fired
5.9	Plane sailing
5.10	The wrong drawing
5.11	Abstract drawing
5.13	Let me tell you a story
5.14	Navigator
5.16	Passing the buck
5.17	What a load of dross
5.18	Strange tools
6.3	Surfing the net
6.7	Rules rules
6.9	The web chain
	✪
3.18	You're great because…
5.12	Magic square

ACTIVITIES IN CREATIVITY ORDER

This table sorts the activities by the creativity star ratings attached to each. Those at the top have the highest star rating, those at the bottom the lowest.

Ref.	Title
	✪✪✪✪
4.7	Handcuffs
5.2	Ands
5.4	Buy me
5.5	Blindfold birthday
5.6	Animals
5.7	Ideas to get you fired
5.8	A to Z
5.9	Plane sailing
5.13	Let me tell you a story
5.14	Navigator
5.15	PR from hell
5.16	Passing the buck
5.17	What a load of dross
5.18	Strange tools
6.5	Fontastic
6.6	Bomb alert
6.7	Rules rule
6.9	The web chain
6.12	Nonsense object
	✪✪✪
4.3	The magic tunnel
4.9	Boy meets girl
4.13	One spare square
5.1	Towering
5.3	Tongue twisters
5.10	The wrong drawing
5.11	Abstract drawing
5.12	Magic square
6.3	Surfing the net
6.4	Snapshots
6.8	Racing demon
6.11	Lego™ construction
	✪✪
3.1	This is my friend

3.2	Tower of Babel
3.4	Something for the weekend
3.5	Follow my leader
3.6	Spoon and string
3.9	True and false
3.10	I am and I know
3.17	You're an animal
4.1	The paper-clip race
4.2	Balloon volleyball
4.4	Bursting with energy
4.5	On the square
4.6	Knots
4.8	Makeover
4.16	Sheepdog trials
4.17	Magic carpet
4.20	Cow tails
4.21	Peer groups
4.22	Giants, witches and dwarves
6.1	People chain
6.2	Contract fishing
6.10	Treasure hunt

✪

3.3	Yes!
3.7	Piggyback plus
3.8	Row of eyes
3.11	Pairing hands
3.12	Keys in the ring
3.13	String in the box
3.14	Trust me, I'll catch you
3.15	Sit on my lap
3.16	Sense and sensibility
3.18	You're great because…
4.10	Steeplechase
4.11	Circle of energy
4.12	Beam me up
4.14	The people machine
4.15	Elastic band race
4.18	Balloon racing
4.19	Out for the count
4.23	Suck and blow
4.24	Magnet race

ACTIVITIES IN FUN ORDER

This table sorts the activities by the fun star ratings attached to each. Those at the top have the highest star rating, those at the bottom the lowest.

Ref.	Title
	✪✪✪✪
3.1	This is my friend
3.2	Tower of Babel
3.5	Follow my leader
3.6	Spoon and string
4.4	Bursting with energy
4.5	On the square
4.6	Knots
4.8	Makeover
4.10	Steeplechase
4.13	One spare square
4.14	The people machine
4.15	Elastic band race
4.16	Sheepdog trials
4.17	Magic carpet
4.18	Balloon racing
4.19	Out for the count
4.20	Cow tails
4.21	Peer groups
4.22	Giants, witches and dwarves
4.23	Suck and blow
4.24	Magnet race
5.1	Towering
5.3	Tongue twisters
5.4	Buy me
5.7	Ideas to get you fired
6.2	Contract fishing
6.4	Snapshots
6.5	Fontastic
6.6	Bomb alert
6.8	Racing demon
6.10	Treasure hunt
6.11	Lego™ construction
	✪✪✪
3.4	Something for the weekend
3.7	Piggyback plus

3.9	True and false
3.10	I am and I know
3.11	Pairing hands
3.12	Keys in the ring
3.15	Sit on my lap
3.16	Sense and sensibility
3.17	You're an animal
4.1	The paper-clip race
4.2	Balloon volleyball
4.3	The magic tunnel
4.7	Handcuffs
4.9	Boy meets girl
4.12	Beam me up
5.2	Ands
5.5	Blindfold birthday
5.6	Animals
5.8	A to Z
5.9	Plane sailing
5.10	The wrong drawing
5.11	Abstract drawing
5.13	Let me tell you a story
5.15	PR from hell
5.16	Passing the buck
5.17	What a load of dross
5.18	Strange tools
6.1	People chain
6.3	Surfing the net
6.7	Rules rule
6.9	The web chain
6.12	Nonsense object

✪✪

3.3	Yes!
3.8	Row of eyes
3.13	String in the box
3.14	Trust me, I'll catch you
4.11	Circle of energy
5.12	Magic square
5.14	Navigator

✪

3.18	You're great because...

ACTIVITIES IN ORDER OF EASE OF PREPARATION

This table sorts the activities by the ease with which you can prepare for them. Those at the top need no preparation, those at the bottom need significantly more.

Ref.	Title
3.1	This is my friend
3.3	Yes!
3.4	Something for the weekend
3.8	Row of eyes
3.9	True and false
3.11	Pairing hands
3.12	Keys in the ring
3.14	Trust me, I'll catch you
3.15	Sit on my lap
3.18	You're great because…
4.6	Knots
4.9	Boy meets girl
4.11	Circle of energy
4.12	Beam me up
4.14	The people machine
4.19	Out for the count
4.21	Peer groups
4.22	Giants, witches and dwarves
5.2	Ands
5.3	Tongue twisters
5.4	Buy me
5.11	Abstract drawing
5.12	Magic square
5.13	Let me tell you a story
5.17	What a load of dross
3.2	Tower of Babel
3.17	You're an animal
4.2	Balloon volleyball
4.3	The magic tunnel
4.5	On the square
4.23	Suck and blow
5.6	Animals
5.7	Ideas to get you fired
5.8	A to Z
5.9	Plane sailing
5.18	Strange tools
3.10	I am and I know
5.15	PR from hell

5.16	Passing the buck
4.1	The paper-clip race
4.4	Bursting with energy
4.15	Elastic band race
4.18	Balloon racing
3.16	Sense and sensibility
4.10	Steeplechase
3.5	Follow my leader
3.6	Spoon and string
3.13	String in the box
4.13	One spare square
4.17	Magic carpet
5.5	Blindfold birthday
4.16	Sheepdog trials
4.20	Cow tails
4.24	Magnet race
5.1	Towering
5.10	The wrong drawing
3.7	Piggyback plus
4.7	Handcuffs
4.8	Makeover
5.14	Navigator
6.5	Fontastic
6.7	Rules rule
6.8	Racing demon
6.10	Treasure hunt
6.12	Nonsense object
6.1	People chain
6.2	Contract fishing
6.4	Snapshots
6.11	Lego™ construction
6.3	Surfing the net
6.6	Bomb alert
6.9	The web chain

ACTIVITIES IN ORDER OF RUNNING TIME

This table sorts the activities by how long they need to run. Those at the top are quicker than those at the bottom. Some activities are dependent upon the team size, so we have assumed a team of around ten for these.

Ref.	**Title**
3.3	Yes!
3.15	Sit on my lap
4.5	On the square
4.19	Out for the count
3.11	Pairing hands
3.14	Trust me, I'll catch you
4.4	Bursting with energy
4.6	Knots
4.18	Balloon racing
5.2	Ands
5.16	Passing the buck
3.2	Tower of Babel
3.4	Something for the weekend
3.6	Spoon and string
3.7	Piggy back plus
3.8	Row of eyes
3.12	Keys in the ring
3.13	String in the box
4.1	The paper-clip race
4.3	The magic tunnel
4.7	Handcuffs
4.9	Boy meets girl
4.10	Steeplechase
4.11	Circle of energy
4.12	Beam me up
4.14	The people machine
4.15	Elastic band race
4.20	Cow tails
4.21	Peer groups
4.22	Giants, witches and dwarves
4.23	Suck and blow
4.24	Magnet race
5.1	Towering
5.3	Tongue twisters
5.5	Blindfold birthday
5.8	A to Z
5.9	Plane sailing

5.10	The wrong drawing
5.11	Abstract drawing
5.12	Magic square
5.14	Navigator
5.15	PR from hell
6.2	Contract fishing
6.7	Rules rule
5.6	Animals
3.5	Follow my leader
3.17	You're an animal
4.2	Balloon volleyball
3.1	This is my friend
3.9	True and false
3.10	I am and I know
3.18	You're great because…
4.13	One spare square
4.16	Sheepdog trials
4.17	Magic carpet
5.4	Buy me
5.7	Ideas to get you fired
5.13	Let me tell you a story
5.17	What a load of dross
5.18	Strange tools
6.1	People chain
6.4	Snapshots
6.5	Fontastic
6.6	Bomb alert
6.8	Racing demon
6.9	The web chain
6.10	Treasure hunt
6.11	Lego™ construction
6.12	Nonsense object
3.16	Sense and sensibility
4.8	Makeover
6.3	Surfing the net